RISE DIVINE EARTH ANGEL

A MAGDALENE SOPHIA ROSE PRAYER PATHWAY OF ASCENSION

LAURA MAVEN STAR

Copyright © 2025 by Laura Hosford and Divine Destiny Publishing.

All Rights Reserved. Apart from any fair dealing for the purposes of research or private study, or criticism or review, as permitted under the Copyright, Designs and Patents Act 1988, this publication may only be reproduced, stored or transmitted, in any form or by any means, with the prior permission in writing of the copyright owner, or in the case of the reprographic reproduction in accordance with the terms of licensees issued by the Copyright Licensing Agency. Inquiries concerning reproduction outside those terms should be sent to the publisher.

DEDICATION

This book is dedicated to Universal Mother Sophia, Mary Magdalene, and Mother Mary, my galactic Light guides, Angels, Sisters, and Brothers of the Rose Grail Pathway. My appreciation to my Mother, Patricia, my first teacher, my grandmothers, and my ancestors for your love and courage. My deepest gratitude to my daughter, Jess, who has walked beside me in this lifetime and others with unconditional love and support. Many blessings to all the beautiful souls, family, friends, and spiritual teachers who believed in me, held me, and inspired me to stay the course and live my brightest angelic starlight again! Blessed Be to All on this pathway of divine love and Light.

CONTENTS

Introduction	ix
Welcome To The Age of Aquarius and the Return of Christ Consciousness	xi

SECTION ONE

The Magdalene - Sophia Living Light Prayer Concepts	3
What Is Ascension: A Return to Original Light	7
How These Prayers Support Your Ascension Pathway	11
How These Prayers Came Into the World	15

SECTION TWO

How Do We Define Prayer?	21
Who Are These Prayers For?	27
Purpose of New Earth Angel's Role and Planetary Mission	31
Benefits of Using this Guide Book as A Spiritual Ascension Pathway	33

SECTION THREE

How to Work With This Prayer Guidebook	39
How to Create Sacred Intentions	43
How to Set Up Your Sacred Alter of Love	49
How to Expand the Living Light Prayer Energies with Ritual	53
Prayer Inquiry Questions to Activate Your Subconscious	57
Post-Meditation Heart Reflections and Integration	63

SECTION FOUR

Guidelines for Working With These Quantum Prayers	67
The Visualization and Activation Process	73
Your Ascension Journey Is Both A Soul Blessing And High Calling	77

SECTION FIVE

How To Call In The Over-lighting Prayer Guides	83
Creating Sacred Space For Your Prayer Practice And Receiving Quantum Healing	85
How To Create A Grounding Cord To Mother Earth	87
A Prayer To Clear Your Chakras and Central Channel	89
Connect with Your Highest Angelic Self and Personal Light Guides	91

SECTION SIX

Ascension Prayer Gateway One	97
Prayer One	109
Ascension Prayer Gateway Two	111
Prayer Two	119
Ascension Prayer Gateway Three	121
Prayer Three	131
Ascension Prayer Gateway Four	133
Prayer Four	143
Ascension Prayer Gateway Five	145
Prayer Five	155
Ascension Prayer Gateway Six	157
Prayer Six	165
Ascension Prayer Gateway Seven	167
Prayer Seven	175
Ascension Prayer Gateway Eight	177
Prayer Eight	185

Ascension Prayer Gateway Nine   187
Prayer Nine   195

SECTION SEVEN

Final Reflections and Summary   199
Glossary of Terms   203
Keep in touch and all offerings   209

About the Author   211

INTRODUCTION

MY STORY

On June 7th, 2017, I boarded a plane to Paris, France. I had no idea my life would be transformed in ways that would echo deep within my Soul. I wasn't just traveling to a new country; I was answering a call that had been growing in my heart for years. Little did I know, this journey would lead me to discover a connection to the land of France, a profound reawakening of my Soul, my purpose, and a deep connection to the Divine Feminine energies that had long been forgotten.

As soon as I set foot on the sacred soil of Southern France, something inside me awakened. It wasn't just the land's beauty or the timeless architecture that captivated me; it was the sweet feminine energy. I felt a deep, almost ancestral connection to something much larger than myself in the rolling hills and ancient caves. I understood that this place was imbued with the energies of the Divine Feminine, the Goddess within, the pure mother energy that has been waiting to reawaken our world.

One afternoon, as I sat meditating in the cave across from Rennes-le-Château, I felt a presence unlike any I had ever experienced before. In that stillness, a vision appeared before me, clear and powerful: the Story of Creation and the return of our Mother God, Sophia. I saw her, radiant and full of grace, coming to restore the Earth's balance and rebuild our world with the energy of unconditional love, peace, and divine creation. At that moment, I knew with every fiber of my being that the return of the Divine Feminine was not a distant dream; it was happening now.

In my vision, Sophia reminded me of the ancient prophecy: the fall of the Divine Feminine had been foretold long before it came to pass. This was all part of the greater plan for humanity's journey. But now, the time had come for the feminine energies to return to the Earth. We were no longer in the dark ages of separation but in an era of reawakening—an era where the nurturing, loving, creative, and healing energies of the Divine Feminine would guide us toward a new world. It was a time of hope, renewal, and profound transformation.

Since March 2008, when in that year, my own life, my own rebirth, you could say, on the priestess pathway, and that's one of the things I'm very passionate about, is helping other women to awaken and remember that they are also a priestess or a goddess. In that year, I received, in total, about 9 downloaded priestess prayers. And so the time has now come with the energies coming in 2025 to really begin to inspire me to put them out into a book and to share them now with you and to share, along with those prayers, my own story of transformation and rebirth that I've been on with the Dark Goddess.

At this time, I discovered a deep, hidden core belief within myself and my family that became a limiting pattern for Soul growth. This ancestral belief was "that change is not possible." If you will, this belief became the fuel to help me move into a new pathway of Soul rebirth and transformation. Today, I can look backward to see how much positive Soul growth has been rooted in my life. Throughout this journey, I've discovered deep inner strengths within my Soul core that have moved mountains in my life.

Today, I'm passionate about helping other women awaken to their inner priestess or Goddess, the pathway of Soul healing, and, in particular, healing the feminine Soul. So, we are all unique individuals. And for me, I have more feminine energy than I do masculine energy, naturally in my Soul makeup. Over the previous centuries, if you were born in a woman's body many times over on this planet and are a feminine Soul, you may have deep, unhealed wounds impacting your life now.

This book is written for those who resonate with that because our feminine Soul's hidden voice wants to rise now. She is the most repressed and creative part of us that yearns to be seen, heard, respected, and liberated fully on this Earth.

She requires us to develop healthy boundaries and the courage to stand up and reclaim our Soul passion to live an inspired life. I want to inspire women to find courage and strength to know they can live as they desire and are no longer repressed.

So, it's really a journey, on a deeper level, of moving out of the inverted feminine and shifting to the enlightened feminine Soul. It is for those ready to reclaim and activate our divine feminine and masculine Christ Light codes in our DNA.

This year, 2025, will be very supportive of the return of the Sophia energies that are coming in now to support our ascension journey of activating our Divine Angelic Soul template. These Magdalene Sophia Prayers of Light are for the ascending new Earth Angel Souls rising now. As a midwife and messenger for the Divine Universal Mother, I remind you that "the goddess is good." That miracles are real, real change is possible for you, and this divine medicine is for inspiring your Soul liberation and illumination.

Years ago, Mother Mary shared this message with me:

> *"I did not come for an ordinary life; these are not ordinary times. I came to liberate your Soul, precious one, so you can be free to come home to your true Mother."*

WELCOME TO THE AGE OF AQUARIUS AND THE RETURN OF CHRIST CONSCIOUSNESS

Prayer to Divine Universal Mother Sophia
"Oh Divine Mother Sophia
I Am In You And
You Are In Me"

Dear Earth Angel,

The Rose is the Heart, and the Magdalene is the Path. Together, they create the New Earth Star reality.

Mary Magdalene is an Earth Angel. She holds the energy of the "Black Madonna" or Earthly Mother Sophia energies. She is the divine template for the Magdalene Pathway, a direct initiatory path into the Grail Mysteries and the embodiment of Christed Love and Sacred Union. It is a path of feminine wisdom, sovereignty, and service to the awakening of humanity.

Tune into your heart, beloved Soul. Do you feel an inner nudge to return home to the Light of your Divinity? To awaken and remember your authentic self that holds your New Earth Angel template. The original Christos-Sophia template for the Divine Human is alive and real. It is happening now in 2025. We are receiving the celestial frequencies of Heaven's Light entering our planet to prepare us for ascension into the New Earth Star timeline in the Golden Age of Aquarius.

Inside this guidebook, you will discover "nine living Light prayers" born from the ancient memory of Light carried in the Earth's breath, the Stars' heartbeat, and the Soul's eternal flame. These prayers have embedded codes and keys to creating inner harmony and peace, Soul embodiment, sacred union, and planetary healing. They are a transmission encoded with Essene purity, Magdalene flame, and New Earth Star Gnosis.

A Magdalene Sophia Prayer pathway to guide, support, and anchor you into the Unity consciousness of Divine Love, also known as the New Earth Star. As you "awaken, align, and anchor" your "I AM" Angelic Soul energies, you become the "sacred rose flame" anchoring Heaven on the New Earth. The possibility of transforming your life experience into greater abundance in your mind, body, and Soul is now supported by our Universal Divine Mother Sophia more than ever in 2025. We are the newly rising Divine Human Angelic Souls, the risen body of the Sophia Christ Consciousness returning to claim our birthright of divine love.

I am so blessed and grateful to be able to share these quantum Light prayers that I received, which are a gift for you from the Universal Divine Mother Sophia's cosmic heart-womb. I am introducing them now (in 2025) because the celestial frequencies of Heaven's Light entering our planet prepare us for ascension into the New Earth Star timeline in the Golden Age of Aquarius.

My heartfelt Prayer for you is to take your time enjoying your prayer pathway journey, allowing time for the energies and Light frequencies to unfold and fully bloom within you with ease and grace. Give yourself permission to fully open your rose heart to receive your divine blessings of abundance, divine love, joy, peace, abundance, harmony, and wholeness. Blessed Be!

SECTION ONE

THE MAGDALENE - SOPHIA LIVING LIGHT PRAYER CONCEPTS

THE MAGDALENE - SOPHIA LIVING LIGHT PRAYER CONCEPTS

This book of prayers is born from the ancient memory of Light carried in the Earth's breath, the stars' heartbeat, and the Soul's eternal flame. Living Light codes are keys to inner harmony, Soul embodiment, and planetary healing. These prayers carry within them the memory of the Essene Path, a way of radiant peace, divine simplicity, and sacred service. As the Essenes communed daily with the Angels of Earth and Heaven, these prayers also restored the divine balance between Soul and creation. They are a transmission encoded with Essene purity, Magdalene flame, and New Earth Star gnosis.

These prayers are not merely spoken. They are living codices, flowing from the Soul's eternal flame and aligned with the sacred traditions of the Magdalene Rose Path and the Essene Way of Light. Rooted in devotion, sovereignty, and divine service, each Prayer is a frequency transmission for personal and planetary ascension into the New Earth Star reality.

In the Magdalene-Rose Path, the heart is the chalice, the voice is the flame, and the body is the temple. These prayers emerge from that same sacred ground where divine feminine and masculine unite, and the Soul radiates through word, breath, and presence. They call forth the fragrance of your Soul Light, awaken your divine Angelic Soul Light, and guide you through the sacred embodiment of love.

Through the Essene remembrance, these prayers also align with the ancient art of speaking Light into form. The Essenes knew that sound and intention could sanctify the Earth, harmonize the body, and prepare the Soul for its greater destiny of service. Each prayer decree reflects that path of honoring the elements, revering Unity, and restoring the original covenant between humanity and Source.

These prayers are not passive requests but active declarations of Light inviting the Higher Self to descend, the ego to serve, and the body temple to become a living Light bridge between Heaven and Earth. As you speak the words of each prayer, you participate in the sacred work of the New Earth Temple Builders, anchoring divine frequencies into the crystalline grid of Gaia and lighting the way for others to remember and awaken.

They are *rose-encoded* affirmations of love, truth, and remembrance. They are *Essene keys* to Soul mastery and planetary healing. They are your words, your breath, your pathway. And they are part of the great unfolding of the New Earth Star within you. May each prayer awaken communion with the Angels of Earth and Heaven and restore the peace within you. May we anchor the New Earth Star through these sacred invocations, awaken the Soul's radiant truth, and serve in Light for the highest good of All.

"And when the sun is high in the heavens, then shall you seek the Holy Stream of SOUND. In the heat of noontide, all creatures are still and seek the shade; the angels of the Earthly Mother are silent for a space. Then it is that you shall let into your ears the Holy Stream of Sound: for it can only be heard in the silence." (excerpt from Edmond Bordeaux Szekely's Essene Gospel of Peace)

WHAT IS ASCENSION: A RETURN TO ORIGINAL LIGHT

Ascension is not about *leaving the Earth* or becoming "more spiritual." It is the progressive remembrance and embodiment of your Divine Origin within the density of form. It is the activation and integration of your multidimensional Self into the living temple of your body, mind, and Soul. It is the reunion of polarities, including Light and matter, Heaven and Earth, divine feminine and masculine, into wholeness within you. Ascension is not a destination. It is a spiral of return from density to divinity, forgetfulness to full remembrance, and separation to oneness lived and breathed.

"You are not becoming Light. You are removing what concealed your Light."

Four Key Pillars of the Ascension Process:

1. **Soul Remembrance**

You awaken to the truth that you are not a being seeking the Divine—you *are* the Divine, remembering Itself in human form. Your Soul contains a Light code (or blueprint) encoded with your purpose, gifts, and divine spark.

2. **Embodiment of Light**

Actual ascension is not escape but the descent of the Soul Light into the physical. The body becomes the altar, the heart becomes the chalice, and your nervous system becomes the throne of the I AM Presence. This is where the Higher Self merges with the human vessel, creating the "Sophia-Christ" human.

3. **Transmutation of Shadow**

As your Light increases, your unmet patterns, pain, and karmic memory surface. These are not signs of failure but gates of initiation. Shadow is not the enemy; it is distorted Light longing to return to its Source. The sacred task is not to destroy the ego but to purify and re-align it as a servant of the Soul.

4. **Sacred Service**

Ascension is not self-centered. It leads to planetary guardianship and Light stewardship. Your awakened presence contributes to the evolution of collective consciousness, Gaia's healing, and the Earth grid's recalibration. As you rise, you emit a frequency, and your Light becomes a song, a signature that guides others Home.

The Human Role in Ascension Is Key

You are not an accidental incarnation. You are a seed of the stars, placed in human form to anchor Light codes into the living body of Earth. Your embodiment *is* the activation, your presence *is* the transmission, and your love *is* the Light.

HOW THESE PRAYERS SUPPORT YOUR ASCENSION PATHWAY

These sacred Light prayers represent a weaving together of living codes, Soul technologies, and vibrational keys to awaken your Angelic-Human template of living divine Light consciousness. They help bridge the human experience with the architecture of the New Earth Star, the emerging 5th-dimensional reality seeded through divine intention and alignment with the Divine Will of birthing Heaven on Earth. These prayers are living blueprints of the New Earth Angel, who is *Unified in love, Aligned in sovereignty, Devoted to the Light, and Anchored in Earth and Spirit.* They give birth to your service, offering, and ascension pathway.

They are designed to be applied as a daily practice of ritual, devotion, purification, and alignment to serve the Light of Creation for personal and planetary ascension and anchor and birth the New Earth Star frequencies. This Magdalene-Sophia pathway "activates" your Soul's remembrance of the contract you made before birth to become the embodied conduit of divine Light and eternal love on this earth plane.

These Heart-Womb prayers of Magdalene Sophia Light support your activation of wholeness, your pure state of divinity, and your internal Christ Consciousness frequency. Mother Mary or Sophia represents this: the "virgin" portal or womb of cosmic creation, the organic state of pure divine feminine love where all life is birthed from the Universal Cosmic Mother of all Creation. She, Sophia, is our true Mother of all life, everywhere.

To awaken into our original state of wholeness, we must purify the dense layers of false beliefs, untruths, distorted imprints, programming, and toxic energies that overlay our true essence of divine angelic perfection. We dissolve and purify out of our sacred temple all "distorted energies" that have created the illusion of separation within us. One prayer at a time, we restore and activate our sacred truth, Soul wisdom, and faith in ourselves to reveal our true nature as divine eternal beings of holy love and pure Light.

There are five primary gateways, and these prayers support your Soul ascension pathway.

1. Activates Soul Remembrance

They affirm your I AM identity, reclaim divine sovereignty, and call forth the Higher Self. This anchors the original Light codes that guide humanity to its eternal truth.

2. Embody Unity and Oneness

These prayers dissolve the illusion of separation between self and Source, human and divine, Earth and cosmos. They recalibrate consciousness into unity frequency, the hallmark of the New Earth Star.

3. Serve as Light Anchors

Each declaration of Light, love, and divine will is an energetic anchor that helps ground New Earth Star frequencies into the planetary grid. As you speak them, you become a living node of Light, a human temple attuned to the New Earth Star ascension timeline.

4. Support the Inner Union

The prayers embody the sacred marriage of Divine Feminine and Masculine within you, Sophia and Logos, Rose and Flame. This balance is essential for ascension, as only a unified vessel can fully hold the New Earth frequency.

5. Transmit Light Codes to Others

As you speak, write, or hold these prayers, their frequency broadcasts through your field. They serve as beacons, calling others into remembrance without words. You become a carrier of Soul Light.

HOW THESE PRAYERS CAME INTO THE WORLD

In July 2015, I received my first downloaded prayer while driving to work one morning. I asked my Higher Self and guides to please hold the download so I could park my car and go inside my office. Whew! This is amazing, and it came in so fast! Within ten minutes, I had my first Sophia Prayer of Light. Then again, in September 2016, Metatron came in to share that I would receive more prayers through my Higher Self and the quantum field. That happened when I downloaded 8 Sophia Prayers of Light in 2016. Seven of the nine prayers in this book were received in 2016 and are now ready to be shared with the world in 2025, as my guides have guided me to do! Over the last nine years, I have received 13 prayers from Sophia Light, holding the Magdalene - Sophia Light Consciousness.

In this prayer book I am sharing nine prayers that support Earth Angels to expand your Light by opening your sacred heart and activating your "I AM" consciousness. These prayers are a golden pathway preparing you for ascension into the New Earth Star. They activate your Angelic DNA frequency of Divine Love. You become more rooted in presence, power, and peace. You are here to anchor in the New Earth Star unity consciousness of Divine love. Each Prayer activates a weaving together of living Light codes, Soul technologies, and vibrational keys to awaken your Angelic-Human blueprint and DNA of living divine Light consciousness.

These quantum prayers of Light and Love are powerful medicine for the ascending New Earth Angel. They invoke divine frequencies to activate your spiritual DNA codes of Divine Love and Unity consciousness. The holy codes of divine love are already held in your DNA to ignite your birthright. To activate your galactic gateway and portal to New Earth Star Unity grid of consciousness or the Zero Point field. The zero point field of Unity consciousness, where Heaven and Earth merge, forms the New Earth Angel Human field of galactic consciousness. These Magdalene prayers restore your divine feminine pathways of Sophia Light in your Celestial Tree of Life, preparing your body complex for merging Heaven and Earth into the unified field of harmony and oneness.

"You do not need to seek the New Earth outside yourself. It exists as a resonance within your Light Body, waiting to be awakened. Align, remember, and step forward into the Eternal Light." "The time is upon you. The portal is open to those who remember. Prepare your vessel, awaken your Light, and step forward through the Eye of the Needle. The New Earth awaits."

The words are the Codes.
Words can light fires in the minds of men.
Words can wring tears from the hardest hearts.
Patricia Rothfuss, writer

SECTION TWO

LIVING LIGHT PRAYERS AS AN ACT OF NEW
EARTH STAR ASCENSION

HOW DO WE DEFINE PRAYER?

Let's take a moment to review how we define "prayer" as a basic foundation for understanding and application of these living prayers of Light. We come from many different backgrounds, countries, cultures, and religions. You do not have to be religious to use this ascension prayer pathway. If you are human, then you are a divine Earth Angel. You are a child of God, the Cosmos, and Mother Earth. You are already holy, sacred, and pure in the eyes of the Divine Source, Mother-Father God, and nothing can change that. You are a precious Soul eternally held and unconditionally loved.

What Is Prayer? The Traditional Definition of Prayer per the English dictionary.

These definitions emphasize devotion, humility, and supplication to a Higher Power, whether personal or universal.

- A solemn request or expression of gratitude directed to God or a divine source.
- A petition or supplication, whether spoken, silent, or inwardly held.
- A set form of words used for invoking spiritual presence.
- An act of spiritual communion encompassing thanks, praise, confession, and reverence.

Now, let's look at what affirmative prayer is.

Affirmative Prayer evolves this understanding into a declaration of divine truth, a co-creative, empowering form of prayer that affirms:

- Agreement with divine will or truth already present
- Emotional support for one's Soul or for others
- A positive, optimistic outlook infused with faith and intention
- Assent in the form of "Yes" to life, to healing, to Source guidance
- Prayer is our direct line with heaven. Prayer is a communication process that allows us to talk to God, the Source.

It is not about asking for something to happen. It is about affirming that it already IS in divine alignment.

Where traditional prayer may say: "God, help me be strong."

Affirmative Prayer says: "I AM one with Divine Strength now."

It is a conscious act of co-creation, rooted in unity with or Organic Creation rather than separation.

Next, let's look at Prayer as an act of Communion.

In both traditions, Prayer is ultimately this: A direct communication with the Divine, a sacred space where the Soul speaks and listens. Prayer is not just asking. It is becoming. It is about the "feeling". Prayer is the language of the Soul, whether in need, joy, or affirmation. It is how we align with the Source, express divine trust, and remember who we are. Prayer can be experienced in many ways, such as:

- A whisper of the heart
- A sung vibration
- A silent knowing
- A wordless surrender
- A deep feeling within

Now, let's look at Living Light Prayers.

- Dynamic: They are not fixed but alive, flowing with divine energy.
- Transformative: They heal, uplift, and re-align with divine order.
- Interconnected: They contribute to a planetary and cosmic weaving of Light.

- Sacramental: They are acts of sacred communion between the individual and the Universal Divine Stream.

Living Light Prayers are dynamic invocations that flow from the fundamental energies of the Universe, embodying pure frequencies of creation. Unlike static prayers, they are living streams of divine energy that heal, uplift, and connect individuals to the Universal Source. Symbolically, they are likened to rays of Light weaving through the cosmos, transforming personal and planetary consciousness.

Most of us were taught to pray in a way that created limiting and conditioned beliefs within us that are not always in alignment with Universal Laws and Truth. Over time, these beliefs may have eroded your ability to connect fully with your divinity and innate Soul power. Although well-intentioned, the prayer practices you learned as a child may not be serving you now to bring about the positive changes you are asking for in your life because of how you were taught to pray. A prayer approach based on the "I am less than (a sinner), I don't have the authority to change my life" concept is taught in most religions. In other words, I must go through an external vehicle to commune with God.

We have given our power and Light to others, organizations, governments, religions, etc. We are caught up believing we are victims, caught in endless experiences of illusion and separation. Now is the time to reclaim your sovereign power as a divine creator in this Universe. We begin that journey today to reclaim your sovereign power, authority, and Soul Light so you may RISE as the powerful Divine Earth Angel that you already are!

So, your life is a living prayer, and how we pray makes a big difference in creating our reality. With the new higher frequencies of consciousness and plasma Light entering Earth, we are quickly becoming master co-creators again with the Divine Source. Our ability to manifest new creations increases as we receive new frequencies of Light plasma. As we embrace our lives as a *living prayer* in motion, we can make new empowering choices as we align with our Angelic frequency. We activate our unique Soul gifts as co-creators with Source. We become more conscious and aware of how our thoughts, words, emotions, and actions impact our lives positively or negatively. How do we contribute to supporting the sacredness of all life or not? You are the designer of your life. As you awaken into your Soul consciousness, taking full responsibility for your unconscious and conscious choices, you align with the Source Creator, becoming a powerful force of divine love.

This living Light prayer guidebook allows you to choose the higher pathway of ascension now in motion on planet Earth. To consciously choose to activate your Angelic Soul frequency, merge with your physical vessel, and become the embodied New Earth Angel in service to the highest good of all beings anchoring Heaven on Earth.

WHO ARE THESE PRAYERS FOR?

Then I asked, "Who are these prayers for?" I was given the name "New Earth Angel." Who are the New Earth Angels?

New Earth Angels are evolved spiritual Light beings or Angelics coming in from the 7th and 9th-dimensional realms who incarnated here into physical form. They were born with a time to awaken through a series of happenings, lessons, or events to awaken to their divine truth. Although they are physical beings, they retain the connection to their higher Angelic counterparts.

These are people whose Soul origins are from beyond Earth and who have spent much time in the higher spiritual dimensions of love and Light. They have an overarching prayer and wish to bring peace, Light, and love to the Earth, humanity, and all beings. Being a New Earth Angel means knowing you are here to serve, love, shine, make a difference, connect with your highest Light, and be a way-shower in choosing this positive timeline of the higher dimensions of love, co-creation, connection, beauty, spirit, and Light.

New Earth Angels are highly spiritually evolved as souls; they vibrate with incredible Light and have been called to Earth on a mission to serve as lighthouses. You're being called now to awaken and remember the Soul dharma that you are uniquely suited to carry out at the Soul level to help others, spread kindness, have compassion, and make a difference on Earth by bringing the Light and love of the higher spiritual realms into physical reality.

New Earth Angels come from every facet of life. You will find them in every country. They come from every race and ethnic background. They may have been raised in a home with religious influences. They work in all industries, corporations, governments, and financial institutions. They are the Angels of God's army waiting in the wings to ride the incoming wave of ascension as the bridge builders of Light, peace, and unity. They hold the Sophia-Christ grail mission of life and Light within their sacred heart. They are here to awaken and remember their Soul contract with the Prime Creator, Divine Mother-Father God, as a catalyst for birthing the New Earth reality. Are you an Earth Angel? The chances are "yes" that you are an Earth Angel led by your Soul in connecting with this book.

New Earth Angels include 144,000 Grail Keepers, Lightbearers, Guardian souls, Stargate holders, Sacred Flame holders,

Lightworkers, Galactic Starseeds, Mary/Isis/Magdalene/Sophia and Rose pathway, The Essenes, Guardians of the Christos-Sophia Grid, Earth Keepers, Light Body Technicians, Indigo, Crystal, Rainbow children and anyone who feels called and aligned with the "Christ - Sophia" Angelic Human template.

As an Indigo child and (Blue Ray) myself, I want to mention those who are also "Indigo children," having come into the planet in the 1950s, 1960s, and 1970s who came first to "break the mold" of the previous third-dimensional structures. Please know you are Highly Intuitive, Strong-Willed, and Innately Wise. You are finely tuned for a different frequency that honors Integrity, Authenticity, and Compassion. You are here to be the shining Lighthouses, unwavering in the storms of change to show humanity a new way of living and being. To co-create the new foundation based on divine love, pure Light, and Unity consciousness for the New Earth Star to RISE. Your time is NOW as the first wave of light-bringers leading us to live authentically, speak our truth, and share our wisdom, building the bridges to the New Earth Star reality. We are awakening and here to remember and celebrate the sacredness and divinity of all life in her original organic form. Blessed Be to all.

PURPOSE OF NEW EARTH ANGEL'S ROLE AND PLANETARY MISSION

New Earth Angels are beings who would act as bridges between realms and carriers of divine frequencies, harmonizers of the Metatronic Light codes, and active participants in the unfolding of the great planetary ascension process. In this role, they are akin to emissaries or avatars of the angelic realms, living in physical form but operating through angelic consciousness.

You are here to become that "bridge of Light" between Heaven and Earth and to anchor your Soul Light into the New Earth Star. You are on an ascension path to evolve spiritually to become "rooted into the 5th, 6th, or 7th dimension." Living as your Angelic Soul Self, you will embody your divine blueprint of Light again, residing from the energies of peace, love, joy, and gratitude. Your mission is to support co-creating the New Earth structures and timeline.

Each Soul contains an "angelic blend," a specific configuration of angelic rays that shape its essence and evolution. These angelic rays are not developed over time but are part of the Soul's original creation. As the Soul evolves, it becomes more aware of and able to commune with these angelic aspects within itself.

New Earth Angels are human souls in the New Earth Star reality who have awakened to their intrinsic angelic lineage. They serve as vessels of heavenly Light, wisdom, and grace, co-creating with divine intelligence and consciousness to elevate the planetary and Soul matrices into the full spectrum of Metatronic Light. They inhabit or work within sacred, spiraling energy temples and serve as teachers, healers, and guides in the New Earth communion of angelic and human domains. You are a rising Divine New Earth Angel if you read this book.

The New Earth Angel's Role in Ascension also includes these qualities within your Soul blueprint.

- Temple Builder: Your body becomes a living cathedral for divine Light
- Grid Worker: Your consciousness interfaces with Gaia's crystalline grid to help stabilize collective evolution
- Light Anchor: You hold higher frequencies steady through devotion, ritual, and right action
- Light Healer: Every inner wound you transmute heals a lineage, uplifts a collective pattern

BENEFITS OF USING THIS GUIDE BOOK AS A SPIRITUAL ASCENSION PATHWAY

Overall, these living Light prayer decrees provide a spiritual pathway for supporting personal growth, accelerating one's spiritual journey during times of ascension, fostering inner peace, and connecting with and embodying your Higher Angelic Soul. They help overcome negative emotions and patterns, bringing them to the surface and into the Light. Enhance your Soul joy and authenticity, expand personal power, and develop your intuition. They support your journey of awakening, how to embrace your sovereignty, heal your emotional issues, and ultimately, embody a more enlightened state. Above all, follow your intuition as your primary inner compass. Allow your Angelic Soul Self to emerge and lead you forward on your ascension journey. Use these prayers with reverence and respect to stay aligned with their healing frequencies. Trust the unfolding of your pathway, staying grounded in love, present and transparent, open to the heart flow of the Goddess's energies to weave a cocoon of divine love in and through you. I have included a partial list of benefits here to get you started.

Benefits of Using this Guide Book for Ascension

- A sacred prayer pathway to accelerate one's spiritual journey into more Light and awareness.
- Teaches you how to create inner peace and calm, contributing to a more serene and balanced state of mind.
- It aids in connecting with one's divine Soul, nature, and authentic expression, fostering a deeper understanding of one's true self.
- Using this guidebook assists in connecting with one's higher self and embodying your Higher Angelic Soul qualities of divine love, peace, harmony, compassion, beauty, joy, and creativity.

Connecting with Divine Guides and Claiming Sovereignty

- Provides a safe sanctuary for connecting with angels and your higher aspects, enhancing spiritual guidance and support for your ascension journey.
- Activating your authentic Soul truth, birthright of sovereignty, and freeing oneself from the past allows for a more present and empowered state of being.
- It aids in healing inner fears, insecurities, anxiety, depression, sadness, worry, anger, and frustration,

promoting emotional well-being and healing of your shadow aspects, lifting you into wholeness.
- Provides self-guided practices in applying living Light prayers to anchor and embody your Angelic Light and sovereignty.

Experiencing Authentic Soul Expression and Expanding Light Body

- Each living Light prayer contains Light codes and key frequencies to align one's authentic Soul expression, allowing for a deeper connection to one's true essence.
- It assists in expanding one's Light body and personal power, enhancing one's ability to manifest one's Angelic Soul mission and express one's Soul gifts into greater world service.
- Expands your Soul intuition, providing greater insight and understanding of spiritual and intuitive messages.
- Awakens your DNA codes of awakening and remembrance of your Divine Soul blueprint.
- It supports connecting all your Lightbody circuits based on your divine Soul blueprint and bringing online your new 5th-dimensional operating system.

SECTION THREE

GETTING STARTED AND GUIDELINES FOR YOUR PRAYER JOURNEY

HOW TO WORK WITH THIS PRAYER GUIDEBOOK

In this prayer guidebook, you will find "nine living light prayers" to support your ascension pathway of activating your divine state of wholeness and Soul Light embodiment for alignment with the New Earth Star timeline and ascension. You will find prayer guidelines with instructions on the application, activation, ritual, and healing potentials. Work with these prayers daily as a spiritual practice, keeping your journal of heart reflections for moments of clarity, inner shifts, unhealed emotions or expressions, and subtle energy movements. Each prayer brings Soul medicine of specific activations, ascension codes, and healing frequencies.

Be fully present with each prayer experience as a partner to support your journey into more soul-love and soul-worth. Give yourself plenty of space and relax into the grace and flow of the prayer medicine. Create your healing affirmations and intentions for specific outcomes and place them on your Sacred Alter of Love. Invite your Higher Angelic Soul, divine Light team, and guides to support your creative outcomes. Make space for the miracles and magic to happen through being "ready, willing and able" to grow and expand your Light. Journal, breathe, sing, dance, draw, and go into nature to invoke the prayer medicine. Let it deepen into communion with your Soul on every level of your being. You are the Priest or Priestess divining with your Soul merging together in divine holy union. You are the lover and the beloved.

You can begin working with each living Light prayer in the sequential order given. Begin with the first prayer gateway, working with its application for three days. Then, you can move to the next prayer gateway, working with its application for three days. And continue to add another new prayer every three days. This will give you an anchored foundation for all nine prayers in 27 days. Then, you can repeat this prayer cycle, moving through all nine prayers, or work with specific prayers as your Soul intuition guides you.

The first three prayer gateways create your new Earth Star foundation. I recommend invoking these three prayers into your daily spiritual practice at a minimum. They are *A Grounding Prayer To Anchor The Magdalene Frequency, A Prayer of Higher Self Embodiment, and Anchoring Divine Heart Light.*

You can then add the other prayers as your Higher Angelic Soul and intuition guide you. You are becoming your embodied Ascended Master Self; part of your mastery in applying these prayers is consistently receiving your Soul's guidance. You can also use this prayer guidebook as an "oracle," tuning into the specific prayer that calls to you.

In each quantum prayer section, you will discover nine gateways of Soul Light medicine.

- Your Prayer Ascension Key Codes
- You're Over Lighting Divine Feminine, Masculine and Angelic Guides
- How each prayer supports your Soul alignment and activation codes of ascension.
- Daily Prayer Mini Activation
- Heart Reflections And Journal Prompt Questions for Reflection
- Ascended Master or Angelic Channeled Message For Ascension Guidance

Specific processes to prepare for your Prayer Pathway Journey for optimal results.

- A set of Prayer Inquiry Questions to Open Your Pathway of Ascension
- How to Set up Your Sacred Altar of Love
- How To Create A Grounding Cord to Mother Earth

- How to Set up your Pyramid of Light Healing Chamber & Trinity Consciousness
- How to create your healing intentions for your highest outcomes
- A Prayer To Clear Your Chakras and Central Channel

HOW TO CREATE SACRED INTENTIONS

At the heart of powerful change is the power of clear, empowered intention as the prime mover of any kind of energetic shift in our reality. All healing journeys start with setting a powerful intention statement. You are the powerful Creator of your life, and learning to direct your energy flow through the power of "intention" is key to creating your desired "outcomes." You get to direct your energy into what you are making, healing, balancing, or resolving. This provides the container or hologram to receive your healing intention. As Divine Earth Angels, we are here to create the new foundation structures for the New Earth Star. As your internal power increases along the ascension pathway, so does what you put your "focus" on, which will begin to manifest more quickly on the Earth. Be clear, be concise, and create from divine love and Light. I always add to the end of my intention statement for my highest good and the highest good of all. This brings your intention into alignment with *the Divine Will*.

What is intention?

Let's start with the dictionary definition:

1. A thing intended; an aim or plan (noun)

2. Medicine: the healing process of a wound

Interestingly, the word intention is linked with healing in its lesser-known meaning.

The intention is an alignment of Heart, Mind, and Body with a clearly articulated outcome. Intention is SOUND as expressed and anchored through the spoken Word. In the ancient texts, the gods were created through the Word. The Word is, and words are, sacred vehicles of Creation, and the fact that we have been given the capacity of speech marks us as creator beings of the highest order. Our clear and aligned intention defines how we co-create with the Earth and all the cosmic forces. Intention is incredibly powerful and one of the fundamentals of our lived experience and, of course, needs to be backed up with consistent and aligned actions.

Your pure intention should be well-thought-out, clear, and aligned with specific desired outcomes. Write out your intention, which grounds it into the Earth's physical plane. Speak your intention out loud so your entire body, heart, womb, and Soul hear it. Write it in your journal. Post it where you can connect with it daily or often. One very clear and powerful intention can serve your spiritual growth for years!

Fun Tips for creating your healing intention statement:

- Connect with your heart space (place one or both hands on your heart and feel warmth)
- Select one of the living Light Sophia prayers in this book and let it speak to you.
- Create a ceremony, Light a candle, walk in nature, and listen to 432hz music to relax.
- Use your favorite Goddesses as guides. Let the words flow from your Soul onto the paper.
- Pull Goddess cards and look at the message. What words appeal to you?
- Envision yourself as the High Priestess or Priest. What qualities do they hold, and include them in your intention statement?
- Visualize the qualities and healing outcome you are creating and draw a picture of the colors, symbols, and words, drawing healing inspiration from it.

Intention Process:

Create your healing intention statement with these beginning words:

My sacred healing intention is to: _____

Heal my relationships with others and create firm, sacred boundaries within and without

Heal my divine feminine wounding

Heal my divine masculine wounding

To heal all co-dependent and victim patterns within myself

To heal all trauma and abuse patterns within myself

To recognize my true Soul nature, I am Soul love, Soul worthy, and I am divine love

Your intention statement should include how you want to FEEL and *the qualities of your Soul's desire.*

I want to feel happy, whole, positive, confident, grateful, joyful, calm, and grounded in my body.

Ask yourself these questions for more clarity:

- *What would my life look like if there were no barriers to my living my dream life? There are no limits here! You are the Creator of your reality! Yes, for real!*
- *What emotions do I want to express more of? Joy, peace, happiness, abundance, flow*
- *What is my greatest need to connect with my feminine self? What does she need more of to thrive?*
- *What is my greatest need to connect with my masculine self? What does he need more of to thrive?*
- *What does my heart-womb want me to know in*

birthing the New Earth's timeline? What is my part to play?

Powerful Affirmations are another way to focus your energy stream of God's particles of Light into the desired outcome you want to create. I always begin my affirmation statements with *"I AM,"* followed by positive and powerful words that anchor in your Soul truth. You can use *index cards* to write affirmations and place them on your Sacred Altar of Love to energize them. You can write them in your Prayer Journal or in a place to see them daily and speak them out loud to the Source Creator. Here are some affirmations that I use myself.

- *I AM a powerful healer and Creator.*
- *I AM the healer of myself.*
- *I AM grateful for my life.*
- *I have the inner Soul knowledge, love, imagination, and divine power to self-heal any condition, trauma, blockage, past, present, and future, to fully allow my divine nature of being of divine love to flow in and through me in every moment.*
- *I believe this with all my heart and Soul because it is my Soul TRUTH! So Be It!*

HOW TO SET UP YOUR SACRED ALTER OF LOVE

For thousands of years, altars have been used in various cultures and religions worldwide to connect people to the higher, unseen worlds of spirit. Although altars may be created for multiple reasons, most are designed to provide a physical, energetic space for healing and deep Soul connection.

It is a sacred space for prayer, reflection, contemplation, and meditation. It is a powerful place to interact with the Goddess's energies to create meaningful rituals and ceremonies and cultivate devotion for your spiritual practice. Creating an altar is a spiritual activity of intention as much as a physical endeavor. Altars can be communal, public, or personal, tucked away from others' curious minds.

When created ceremoniously and in ritual, your altar is a place for sanctuary, prayer, meditation, and ritual. It is a place to hold your prayers and intentions and focus your love and connection to the Spirit. *An altar is a place of non-ordinary reality held within ordinary reality.* Altars are for your spiritual mind and Soul's heart to merge with your personality. Whether communal or personal, altars help to anchor your focus on Spirit, love, faith, and devotion and bring in new creative possibilities for your spiritual journey.

Creating Your Own Personal Altar

I love setting up new altar spaces! Make it fun and easy. Get into your creative Soul's flow! Set aside a private place in your home to set up your personal altar. It doesn't have to be large. It can be as small as your bedside table or even the drawer of your bedside table.

1. Clear it of all clutter. Find a beautiful scarf, cloth, or covering that is beautiful and feels sacred to you. This will help set the sacredness of the space.
2. At the center of the altar, place a small statuette, piece of art, crystal, flowers, cards, or an item representing the Spirit, Goddess, God, or the Universe.
3. Place a candle on the altar. Use your intuition as to where it belongs
4. You can place other items on the altar, such as flowers, crystals, a small chalice of water, feathers, and sand.
5. Select a theme for your altar. The items you place on the altar should bring love, beauty, and honor to the Spirit and Divine Mother and integrate with your intentions.

6. Smudge your altar with palo santo, sage, cedar, sweet grass, or whatever combination of herbs you are called to use. Dust it physically to keep it as clean energetically as you do.

Preparing for Your Altar Work

Take time each day to sit at your altar, focusing on the Spirit through your heart, prayers, gratitude, and intentions. When you sit, you can burn incense and play music to assist you in going inward to connect to your intuition and to the Spirit or a Goddess you want to invoke healing energies with. Create more sacred space with prayers, chants, or through meditation. When you are quiet and focused, you begin to open to the messages and healing energies the Spirit has for you. Keep a journal at your altar to write down the messages and wisdom you receive from your Higher Self and Soul or Higher Guide.

Prayer and Invocation

Enter into prayer mindfully, centered in your heart with gratitude. Light your candle, and send your prayers to the Spirit in your mind, heart, and words. Pray gratefully with an earnest heart, opening to the love and gifts available to you. Visualize your prayers as not only heard but answered.

Let go of outcomes and be open to Spirit's larger vision for you and your life. Open to greater possibilities, expressing yourself from Great Mystery, and answering your prayers in love beyond what your human mind can grasp. Spirit works in the mystery and ultimately weaves a path of awakening when you surrender and trust the Greater Spirit and interconnectedness of life. Making an altar and practicing prayer, ritual, and gratitude mindfully can heal your life beyond anything you can imagine. It brings peace with focus through the heart. This ancient practice of prayer and altar work anchors your prayers from earth to heaven and heaven to earth in a tapestry of woven intentions that are your heart song.

HOW TO EXPAND THE LIVING LIGHT PRAYER ENERGIES WITH RITUAL

You can create your own ritual ceremonies with each living Light prayer to deepen, expand, and anchor the energies. Here is a ritual template that will get you started. Then, using your unique creative energy and ideas, begin to create your own rituals. Let this be playful and fun as our highest Light guides love to connect with us through the heart of our inner child energy.

What You Need:

- A white candle that represents purity and divine connection
- Choose one or more crystals such as Rose Quartz, Selenite, Amethyst, Clear Quartz
- A cup or chalice of water that represents emotional purification

- A bowl of sand or soil that represents grounding into Mother Earth

Step-by-Step Ritual

1. Set Up Your Sacred Space

- Light the white candle and place a chalice of pure water and soil before you.
- Connect with your "I AM" Self by touching your heart center.
- Invite in the overlighting divine feminine, masculine, and Angelic guides for the specific prayer you are invoking.
- Chant the word "OM" three times to invoke unity
- Place your crystals on your altar or in front of you.
- Place your left hand on your heart and the other on your womb or lower belly.

2. Speak the Prayer Out Loud Three times

- Read each line with full intention, pausing after each line to let the words anchor into your heart and womb or lower belly.
- Speak your prayer intentions out loud, activating your chalice of water and bowl of soil.

3. Breathe in the Illuminated Light

- Close your eyes and visualize ruby-gold Angelic rays of Light spiraling around and through you.
- See and feel your heart chakra blooming open like a rose filled with white-gold crystalline Light.

4. Sealing the Prayer Activation

- Now, say out loud, "I AM Soul Grounded." Place your right hand on the bowl of soil.
- Then say "I AM Soul Feeling" out loud, and drink your chalice of water to integrate emotional wisdom.
- Write down the prayer on a piece of paper.
- Hold it in both hands and say: "I seal this declaration into my soul. It is done!"
- Burn the paper (fire release) or bury it in the Earth (grounding into reality).

5. Closing & Gratitude

- Thank your Divine Guides and Angels for witnessing your Soul Activation.
- Let the candle burn out naturally.
- Keep your crystal with you for seven days to continue anchoring the prayer's energy.

Optional Ways to Expand the Energy Frequencies

- Create your intention statement and place it on your sacred altar, speaking this prayer over it.
- Place fresh red roses or the color you like on your sacred altar.
- Place a chalice of water on your sacred altar, and say this prayer over it to cleanse your emotions.
- Work with crystals (amethyst), water, or essential oils (rose, frankincense) to anchor the energy.
- Practice grounding techniques (walking in nature, deep breathing) to balance your expanded state.
- Use it before or after energy healing, meditation, or spiritual work.
- Make a voice recording of your prayer and intention statement out loud for your daily practice.

PRAYER INQUIRY QUESTIONS TO ACTIVATE YOUR SUBCONSCIOUS

As you activate the specific Light frequencies of each prayer, you will notice subtle shifts in your energy field. This requires shifting your focus "inward," bringing your energy into a state of relaxation, calm, and deep presence. You are learning to tune into the "inner stillness" found within you that is your Soul energy. This may take time if you are not currently meditating or have a practice of contemplation. So, be gentle and patient as you learn to open up space inside you for a dialog with your Soul. Your experiences will vary as you deepen into each prayer's energies. The best mindset is to be open and willing to allow space within for you to receive messages, shifts in energy, unexpressed emotions, hidden beliefs, or old stories to rise to the surface of your consciousness.

Keep a prayer journal near your sacred space to write down your observations, insights, and shifts, and track your beliefs, stories, perceptions, emotions, and feelings about yourself and others. As your Soul Light expands, so does your "awareness" of coming into a more profound clarity of your current world reality. Everyone has their own "internal lens" and filters of how they perceive the world. In your prayer journal, always describe your experience of feeling, hearing, seeing, sensing, or knowing after invoking each prayer. Each quantum prayer invites you into a deep state of "stillness" and "presence" of "inner communion" within your body and Soul.

Write down all rising inner beliefs coming to the surface of your consciousness that do not match your external reality patterns to see where alignment is needed. Ask for alignment in all areas of your life to match your "original divine soul blueprint" that resides eternally in the heart of Creation. Create powerful intention statements to align you fully with complete Soul embodiment in your physical vessel and activation of your "soul song," which is your unique Angelic Soul frequency of love-light.

Answers, solutions, and moments of clarity are sparked from within you as you expand your Soul Light field. You may also receive deep insights through your dream time, spending time in nature, contemplation, and meditation. Write down everything that comes to you and trust it has come in for your highest guidance. This is important as you build up your Soul intuition by receiving messages and taking new actions to support your ascension pathway with more ease, grace, and fun! Open up space for your ability to "trust" yourself every step of the way, knowing that the Divine Source of all life is always lifting you up!

Here is a sample list of questions for your deeper inquiry and experience working with each Light prayer.

Please show me something I don't know to facilitate the healing of myself today.

What am I sensing and feeling when I read and tune into the energies of this prayer?

How does my body feel when I read this prayer?

Is there an emotional connection to this prayer?

Where do I feel the expansion of Light in my body?

Describe your experience of this prayer?

Do I feel my crown chakra opening? My heart chakra opening?

What is my overall state of self-love and self-connection in my body?

Which parts of my body am I more connected with? Less connected with?

Do I feel my heart, throat, and womb/lower belly as centers of power?

Do I feel grounded and safe in my body?

Do I feel calm and present in my body?

What unexpressed thoughts, beliefs, or stories are rising within me?

What emotions or feelings do I sense with this prayer?

What does my body want me to know?

What does my divine Light team want me to know about my Soul today?

Who is my guardian angel?

Who are my primary divine feminine guides?

Who are my primary divine masculine guides?

My divine guides would like for me to bring in more _____ in my life.

I want a spiritual breakthrough, and I ask my divine Light helpers and healers to support me in partnership for my highest healing and transformation.

Show me where I have unhealthy attachments in my life.

Show me where I am projecting my unhealed emotions or wounds onto others?

Show me my unhealed patterns, ready to be seen, felt, and healed.

Where is my mind in chaos or conflict?

Where am I at battle within myself? My body? My mind? My emotions?

Please show me hidden patterns, beliefs, or stories, anchoring me in third-dimensional consciousness.

POST-MEDITATION HEART REFLECTIONS AND INTEGRATION

After each prayer meditation, tune into your feelings and notice what has shifted? What has come to your conscious awareness to be felt and embraced with divine love? Perhaps a moment of clarity or an "aha." Write everything down that you experienced in your meditation. Tune inward into the stillness and be with it entirely.

- A deep sense of oneness and inner peace
- Heart expansion and increased love for all beings
- A stronger connection to your I AM Presence and divine purpose
- A heightened ability to radiate divine Light into the world

SECTION FOUR

PRAYER GUIDELINES FOR QUANTUM SOUL HEALING

GUIDELINES FOR WORKING WITH THESE QUANTUM PRAYERS

To receive and activate the inner transformation and powerful shifts you want to create, use these prayers daily as a spiritual practice. As you consistently connect with each Prayer's energy codes and frequencies, they begin working with your DNA at deep levels. Light codes of the Universal Mother Sophia activate new levels of Unity consciousness within you. Each prayer holds the "divine love" frequency of the Divine Mother Universal consciousness. Also, it is charged with "Light Language frequencies" of Divine Love & Light consciousness, forming a sacred geometry.

The purpose of these prayers is to guide you into fully aligning yourself with the New Earth Star Vibration of Unity Consciousness or Christ Consciousness, to anchor in a new foundation of life, and to live in divine love consciousness as a fully ascended Angelic Soul.

As you sit with each prayer, *allow it to reveal its magic to your heart deeply by "feeling" into it.* These living Light prayers open doors to creation, creating a New Earth's Star hologram and foundation for your Angelic Soul consciousness. As you consciously align with the New Earth's vibration of Divine Love and Unity, you also agree to live in alignment with the Law of One.

- Find a quiet, comfortable place to begin your prayer practice. Set up your sacred altar of Love to create your chalice for receiving energy and supporting your prayer intentions.
- Purify your space with sage or palo santo. Light a white candle to attract your divine team of Light.
- Have your prayer journal and pen for receiving messages and reflections.
- Take a lying or seated position. Close your eyes and connect to your body through deep belly breathing. Breathe into the count of four through your nose. Then slowly exhale out your mouth, feeling your breath like a beautiful liquid Light washing through your heart, womb chakra, or lower belly and out your root chakra. Become aware of the color and feeling frequency of this Light. Repeat this process for 3 to 5 breaths until you feel relaxed and centered in your body.
- As you breathe out, imagine releasing all of your anxiety and stress out of your body, sending it down into the crystalline heart-womb core of New Earth.

- Place one hand on your heart center to connect with your "I AM" presence and one hand on your womb or lower belly. This will help anchor your unique flow of "I AM" Soul Light particles into your primary chakras. You become the embodied vessel or bridge of Light between "Heaven and Earth."
- Speak the words of each prayer out loud (three times) with confidence and presence, pausing to *feel* the meaning and spirit of each prayer's frequencies. These are subtle frequencies.
- As you read each prayer out loud, speak it slowly with your "focused attention." Drop into the "feeling tones" of the prayer, noticing and observing where you feel an opening or expansion of Light and energy flowing in your body. You will feel this expansion primarily in your seven major chakras. You may also feel it within your womb chakra or lower belly.
- As you *feel the energy*, you are building up Light momentum within you. Continue to let the Light expand within you. As you feel this deep connection expanding within your heart and Soul, the prayer becomes a meditation as you commune with your "I AM" presence each day.
- As you read each prayer with deep devotion, you are "invoking" and "activating" the energy codes embedded within each prayer. Open your heart chakra to receive the quantum energy flow of Light coming through to you. After you have completed saying the prayer out loud, close your eyes and *feel* your

connection within your heart space and your own "I AM" presence and response.

- The prayer position you will use for all prayers unless otherwise stated is: One hand on the heart and the other hand on the womb or lower belly/dantien. This position naturally connects you to the cosmic heart of Universal Divine Mother Sophia and flows into the zero-point field. This is the Heart-Womb Gateway through which Light descends into density. You become the conduit or bridge anchoring Heaven's Light to Earth.
- After reading the prayer and completing the meditation, sit in silence for 10 to 20 minutes, allowing the Light frequencies within the words to fully integrate and expand within your aura and chakras and into your mental, emotional, spiritual, and physical bodies.
- As your personal Light quotient increases and builds within your body and aura, it will expand into deeper levels of your subconscious, igniting unexpressed or unhealed emotions, parts of your unhealed shadow self, and false or limiting beliefs, stories, or untruths that rise in your consciousness for integration into a state of wholeness. This process is accelerated during ascension as the cosmic universe supports us in purifying our energy bodies of repressed emotions and unhealed wounds or shadow parts.
- Keep a journal to write down the messages you receive, divine inspirations, downloads of energy,

inner shifts in perception, aha moments of clarity, and breakthroughs. As you focus on expanding your Soul Light and vibration, you integrate it with your physical body temple. This is the sacred union of bringing "spirit into matter," the holy union.
- Optional. You may want to use "mala beads" with your prayers to build the Light energy within each prayer. Each prayer creates a "trinity effect" to align with the New Earth Star timeline. Hence, each prayer equals "12 mala beads." Nine prayers times 12 beads equals 108 beads.

Note: I do not recommend using a prayer rosary because it is not in alignment with these prayers.

THE VISUALIZATION AND ACTIVATION PROCESS

These prayers contain several levels and hidden layers of "activation energies," which means "to make active, alive and cause to function." There are specific activations for your chakras and to activate particular frequencies for the Soul's divine presence, embodiment, and higher consciousness embodiment. Each prayer affirms an aspect of your *Soul mastery, integrating the higher self into physical reality. (Please note it was impossible to include all prayer activations since there are many levels and layers, but you can experience more in my Earth Angel Sophia Sanctuary online circle.)*

Read and follow the instructions listed for each prayer. Read the prayers out loud (three times) and then do the visualization or activation followed by 10 to 20 minutes of quiet inner reflection and journaling. Keep a prayer journal to record your "insights," including thoughts, beliefs, emotions, feelings, stories, and moments of "clarity" rising within you. As you invoke the Light frequencies of each prayer working in alignment with Divine Mother Sophia's rays of plasma Light particles now showering our planet, you create a "frequency match" to activate your original angelic Soul blueprint.

The more pure Divine Love you generate within your feeling world, the sooner you will notice the transformation for yourself and the world around you. Everything in the Universe is made of Light particles, including Prayers and Affirmations, tools to invoke Light frequencies and awaken more spiritual DNA already held within you.

If you desire to ascend and live in the Realms of Love and Light, it is essential to increase your Light quotient daily. We came from the Light and are destined to return to the Light. This is divine truth from The Law of One. If the Soul desires to fully ascend and live in the Heavenly Realms of Love and Light or the New Earth Star of Unity consciousness, make time daily to invest in your soul's ascension process. All of life was birthed out of the Universal Divine Mother Sophia's cosmic womb of creation. It is your destiny to return to the unified source of all life and become fully reunited with your "I AM" presence, living in harmony, peace, and self-love state of consciousness.

Also, not everyone will "see or visualize" the Light flowing into your body and aura. Depending on your natural energy flow and psychic gifts, you may receive and perceive "light" in other ways, such as feeling, sensing, hearing, knowing, or through your imagination. All of these ways are valid. Trusting and following your intuition is key to your ascension pathway. Bring these living Light prayers into your spiritual practice to support the expansion of your multi-dimensional self and Soul embodiment.

YOUR ASCENSION JOURNEY IS BOTH A SOUL BLESSING AND HIGH CALLING

There are *nine Sophia Prayers of Light* to support your ascension pathway of awakening on your Soul journey to embody your Angelic Frequency of divine love and Light, living in your authentic "I AM" trinity of wholeness state.

Each prayer holds a specific intention and vibrational frequencies you work with to activate, align, and integrate within your energy bodies. This includes expanding your embodied consciousness and light quotient or vibrational frequency. As you work with these prayers consistently, they build up your new vibrational foundation of Soul Light, guiding you to anchor and embody your New Earth Star reality fully.

The I AM is the bridge that opens the doors to all dimensions, the gatekeeper to all inner energy gateways, and the connector between all parts of you. It gathers all your inner voices and aspects and leads them to wholeness. The I AM is the one central pillar and guide of all parts of you and illuminates all parts of you. Immersing in the I AM activates your Angelic Soul Song of Light.

The power of these words, *"I AM,"* is *equivalent to turning on a Light switch inside you*. They activate the God particles of pure Light potentials for creation within you. Use them carefully to create your New Earth reality foundation, always aligning with your Soul values of love and worth. Use these words to make affirmation statements based on divine truth that uplifts, heals, and inspires your reclamation of whole Soul embodiment and your original divine human, angelic state of wholeness. Your ability to co-create is increasing daily as you embody more of your Soul Light into your physical body or temple. Choose your thoughts, words, beliefs, stories, feelings, and actions carefully. You are given a great responsibility to "birth" in the New Earth reality with divine love and respect and for the highest good of all life forms. This is a high calling. Are you ready to soar?

You are part of the eternal flow of life. And all of life is birthed out of the holy womb of Divine Universal Cosmic Mother Sophia as a pure stream of consciousness. This is the great womb of Sophia, the Mother of all creation that holds and gives birth to all life. She is the original creator, before sound and manifest Light from which all life originates. This is the divine truth; everything is sacred. Your Soul is already sacred, pure, and holy. Therefore, you are fully ordained with divine authority as an Ambassador of God's Light to return to your original state of Soul perfection while embodied on planet Earth. This is your wake-up call to return to the Light of your Soul and rise into eternity now.

SECTION FIVE

CREATING YOUR PYRAMID OF LIGHT AND WORKING WITH LIGHT GUIDES

HOW TO CALL IN THE OVER-LIGHTING PRAYER GUIDES

Your Over-lighting Divine Feminine and Masculine Guides

You will find a set of "over-lighting" divine feminine, divine masculine, and Angelic guides for each living Light prayer. Each Prayer activates specific energy frequencies and sacred geometries on your ascension journey. Feel your Soul journey as a "rose spiral," opening new inner gateways of remembrance and connection with each over-lighting Light guide. Set a playful intention to open space for two-way communication with each Light guide and for it to flow with "ease and grace." Our highest Light guides love being playful and creative and having fun and laughter! Be creative about the best way for you to connect. Also, it is essential that you always approach all Light guides, including Angels, Archangels, Ascended Masters, Goddess energies, or Galactic energies, with respect and that you are their "equal." You are not above or below them. You are a sovereign divine being.

Call on one or more of these divine Light guides while invoking each prayer to support your pathway of Soul ascension at every step. Use your intuition to guide you when to play with a particular Light guide. You can use your Sacred Altar of Love to invoke the energies of a specific Light guide by placing an image or crystal aligned with their energy. These Light guides represent part of your Angelic Over-soul team, guiding you home to a full reunion with your true Cosmic parents and "I AM" Angelic Soul.

CREATING SACRED SPACE FOR YOUR PRAYER PRACTICE AND RECEIVING QUANTUM HEALING

Let's get started! Now, you are ready to begin activating, aligning, and anchoring in your beautiful, radiant Angelic Soul essence, which I call your "Angelic Soul Song." This divine spark or sacred flame holds your original Soul blueprint made by the Prime Creator or Mother-Father God energy. You are an "original," and no other divine spark is like you! So, in your most authentic state of being, you are like a "diamond shining without limitations" in the cosmos. You, dear one, are a very bright diamond starlight!

First, read the *Guidelines for Working With These Quantum Prayers (see previous section)* to learn how to use these Prayers for optimal results.

Second, complete these practice steps before you begin your prayer meditations to help you become centered, relaxed, and focused *on receiving Soul* healing and transformation.

1. Find a quiet, comfortable place to begin your prayer practice. Set up your sacred altar of Love space to create your chalice for receiving energy and supporting your prayer intentions.
2. Purify your space with sage or palo santo. Light a white candle to bring in the Light. Prepare a glass of pure water and place it on your altar. Add fresh flowers or crystals of your choice. Have your prayer journal and pen to receive messages and reflections.
3. Take a lying or seated position. Close your eyes and connect to your body through deep belly breathing. Breathe into the count of four through your nose. Then, slowly exhale out your mouth, feeling your breath like a beautiful liquid Light washing through your diaphragm, belly, womb, and root chakra. Become aware of the color, feeling, or frequency of this Light. Repeat this process for 3 to 5 breaths until you feel relaxed and centered in your body.
4. Next, create your grounding cord. (Page 87)
5. Now, you can clear and balance your nine chakras and central channels. See below A *Prayer To Clear Your Chakras and Central Channel*. (Page 89)
6. Your final step is to create your *Pyramid of Light Healing Chamber and Trinity Consciousness* to complete your preparation. (Page 91)

HOW TO CREATE A GROUNDING CORD TO MOTHER EARTH

Payfully imagine (see, feel, hear, or sense) an emerald green ball of spinning Light inside your "root chakra" at the base of your spine. Let it spin, then fall into the center of the Earth, creating a cord or tube of emerald green Light rooting into the heart-womb crystalline core of Mother Earth. Feel your ball of spinning Light expand and merge, becoming one with the "heart-womb" of Mother Earth. You may feel a slight magnetic pull downward, resting or relaxing into her core. You may feel warm or calm or very present. You may feel your heart chakra open after you ground into Mother Earth. Feel a wave of her unconditional love inside your heart and body, embracing you with gentleness and grace. The purpose of creating your grounding cord is to flow excess energy out of your aura, supporting your body to feel safer and more comfortable.

A PRAYER TO CLEAR YOUR CHAKRAS AND CENTRAL CHANNEL

I open my God mind,
I open my Sacred Heart.
I call my God Light into my vessel.
I allow it to be
I ask for complete clarity,
to see perfectly, to speak wisely, and to receive with purity.
My vessel is pure diamond Light and is now ready to receive.
So be it, and So it is. It Is Done!

- Set your intention that all nine chakras and the central channels (your spiritual spine) be purified, cleansed, and balanced to align with the fifth-dimensional field of Unity and Divine Love frequency.
- Say this Prayer out loud three times with one hand on your heart and the other on your womb or lower belly.

- Using your imagination, see or feel a higher vibrating, crystalline diamond platinum Light, as spirals of Light, a swirling vortex coming down from the highest skies above you, entering about 18 inches above your head, opening your Soul Star chakra. It moves downward entering your crown chakra (top of head), into your third eye (center of your head), into your throat, center of your heart, into your solar plexus (above your belly button), then your sacral (below your belly button), then into your root chakra (at the base of your spine) and down into the Earth Star (below your feet) cleansing, purifying and dissolving all energies not in alignment with your Angelic Soul divine blueprint.

CONNECT WITH YOUR HIGHEST ANGELIC SELF AND PERSONAL LIGHT GUIDES

Pyramid of Light Healing Chamber & Trinity Consciousness

This universal quantum container acts as your sacred container for transmutation and transformation and supports your vibrational shifts into higher consciousness. It also provides "psychic protection" of unseen forces at play so you can fully open into a safe sanctuary container you can trust, grow, and evolve your frequency. You will create a *Pyramid of Light Healing Chamber & Trinity Consciousness container to support your Soul expansion and consciousness into a new embodiment frequency.* You will call in your Higher Self and divine Light guides to develop your Trinity Consciousness container. This pyramid of Light includes your Higher Self and divine Light guides, including angelic frequencies.

- Connect with your Sacred Heart space by placing two fingers on your heart center and feeling your heart softening and opening within. You might feel a sense of warmth, tingling, or inner expansion. You can gently rub small circles with two fingers on your heart center. Place your other hand on your womb or lower belly center.
- Playfully imagine (see, feel, hear, sense) a pyramid of pure white and golden Light expanding inside your sacred heart center.
- Invite your Higher Angelic Self and divine Light guides to join you in your pyramid.
- Relax and ask your higher angelic self and personal Light guides to fill your pyramid of Light, weaving together your pure Light God particles with your highest guides' energy, raising the frequency of your pyramid of Light to the "fifth dimension or higher."
- Empty your mind of all thoughts and become aware of the "inner stillness" within your pyramid of Light container.
- Open to receive messages and higher guidance and healing Light frequencies.
- Now expand your pyramid of golden Light outward from your heart until it forms around your body and aura, creating a cocoon of divine love and warm Light embracing your whole body, crown, third eye, heart, womb, and lower belly in a safe sanctuary.
- Open your heart and intuition with "feeling," your inner sight. See or sense images or colors, hear

positive words, feel goosebumps or tingles, and feel warm, safe, and grounded. You have prepared a space to "receive your healing and transformation."

"To Thine Own Self Be True" -Oracle of Delphi

SECTION SIX

MAGDALENE - SOPHIA PRAYERS OF LIGHT
PATHWAY

ASCENSION PRAYER GATEWAY ONE

HEAVEN ON EARTH: ANCHORING THE NEW EARTH STAR

A Grounding Prayer To Anchor The Magdalene Frequency
Five Pointed Star

Ascension Key Codes: Root and Womb Chakra Healing • Magdalene Grail Flame • Holy Feminine Presence

The Feminine Prayer Medicine

This prayer anchors your "I AM" Angelic Soul Self as a "bridge of light" between Heaven and New Earth Star. You anchor the Magdalene Light Codes frequency and divine feminine wisdom into the New Earth Star and 44:44 Ascension gateway. This is true, Hieros Gamos, uniting spirit with matter within. You transcend linear time, moving through the Stargate into divine service to All That Is, which activates your

Soul's mission in planetary ascension. This sacred prayer bridges Earth and the Cosmos, anchoring your being in divine alignment with the physical and celestial realms. It is a divine activation decree, balancing grounded embodiment with higher-dimensional Light body expansion. It activates and grounds in your *Root Chakra*, stabilizing your connection to the crystalline core of *the New Earth Star*.

Invoking this prayer awakens the Goddess within you, connecting you to the divine mother, cosmic wisdom, and the path of Light service. You embody the Rose Codes of Magdalene, the wisdom of Sophia, Isis's strength, Quan Yin's compassion, and Gaia's grounding presence. These Light codes may awaken within you a deep mystical remembrance of your Soul pathway as a Magdalene Rose Priestesses (of Love and Light), Isis Mystery School lineage (of higher Consciousness and ascension), or midwife for the Cosmic Sophia Codes (of Divine Light and Creation).

The Frequency of the Rose is one of the most sacred and subtle vibrations in all creation, a living tone of divine remembrance, unconditional love, and holy beauty. To feel it is to remember Sophia's womb, Mary Magdalene's heart, and the Sacred Mother's breath in all her forms. It is the vibration of the Grail, the Path of Love, and the unfolding Soul.

This prayer is a divine invocation that bridges the celestial and earthly realms. It carries the frequency of the Divine Feminine in her many aspects, activating different Goddess energies that correspond to sacred wisdom, ascension, and the embodiment of divine love. It supports embracing and remembering your Divine Feminine Power, activating multiple divine feminine frequencies and key codes for full Soul embodiment. You are the Light Bearer and living Light bridge accessing Sophia's celestial wisdom anchoring into the heart-womb crystalline core of Gaia's womb of the New Earth Star. You are the living embodiment and bridge between Heaven and Earth, anchoring your "I AM" Angelic Soul light-love presence into physical matter. This is a sacred initiation into your Soul's highest path!

"Embrace Your Divine Feminine Power as you are a living epistle of the Way of Love. YOU are the Creator of your experience. If you shift your inner world, your outer world must follow. Align with love, and love will align with you. Heal within, and the world around you will transform."

Your Overlighting Divine Feminine and Masculine Guides

Call on these divine guides while invoking this prayer to support your pathway of Soul ascension every step of the way. They represent part of your Angelic Over-soul team guiding you home to a full reunion with your true Cosmic parents and "I AM" Angelic Soul.

The Gaia-Sophia Archetype includes a trinity of feminine energies: Earthly Mother and Mary Magdalene, Cosmic Mother Sophia and Isis, and Mary Magdalene and Quan Yin.

Archangel Metatron Archetyps: Metatron and Archangel Michael

Divine Feminine: The Great Womb of Gaia-Sophia

- Embodied Archetype: *Gaia-Sophia*, the primal feminine intelligence of Earth, the one who sings your bones into form. The Archetype of Gaia-Sophia is one of the most primordial and encompassing Divine Feminine streams in esoteric cosmology. She is not a single goddess but a symphonic consciousness woven from many great goddess energies across mythic, planetary, and cosmic traditions. Gaia-Sophia is the Living Earth Intelligence merged with Celestial Wisdom. She brings holding, nurturing, grounding, safety, grace and compassion.
- Qualities invoked in this Prayer: Deep somatic trust, she reminds you that to rise, you must root into her womb, anchoring your Soul into the planetary ascension path. The trinity of feminine energies supports your Soul's evolution into divine sovereignty and sacred service.

Divine Masculine: The Cosmic Pillar of Metatron

1. Embodied Archetype: *Archangel Metatron* opens the stargates of time and aligns your divine blueprint. (Sacred Geometry and Higher Consciousness). *Archangel Michael*, as you declare your readiness to serve, Michael strengthens your path in divine service. (Protection and Light Service)

2. Essence: Ascension, clarity, divine order, celestial vision
3. Qualities invoked in this Prayer: Clear direction and intention, the "Yes" to purpose in sacred service

A Prayer Ritual Activation for Grounded Embodiment and Higher-Dimensional Light Body

Speak It Daily to activate your "feminine trinity."

This trinity of feminine energies supports your Soul's evolution into divine sovereignty and sacred service.

- Say this prayer out loud three times while placing one hand on your Heart and the other hand on your Womb/lower belly
- Create your intention statement and place it on your sacred altar, speaking this prayer over it
- Place a chalice of water on your sacred altar, speaking this prayer over it to cleanse your emotions
- It activates a "feminine trinity," weaving together three key divine feminine archetype energies.

Heart and Root Chakra Activation Meditation:

- As you say each line, imagine a radiant five-pointed star spinning in rose-gold Light at your heart. Let it expand gently throughout your womb/lower belly, then into your root chakra and aura, anchoring into the crystalline heart-womb core of the New Earth Star.

Offer Sacred Rituals:

- Light a candle and speak your prayer aloud three times in devotion to the sacred feminine.
- Place flowers (roses, lotus, or jasmine) on your altar.
- Use anointing oils like frankincense and myrrh to bless your energy field.

Chant Goddess Invocations:

- "Sophia, Isis, Magdalene, Gaia, Quan Yin, I call upon your presence now."

Meditate with their energies:

- Envision them encircling you in divine Light as you recite your prayer.
- Ask them to reveal their guidance through dreams and synchronicities.

Write It on Paper And Place It On Your Altar:

- Place it on your altar, mirror, or journal as a daily reminder of your divine embodiment.
- Place an image of each Goddess on your sacred altar to anchor their energy in your field.

Ways to Honor Earth Mother in This Prayer:

- Meditate barefoot on the Earth to strengthen this connection.
- Offer a small token of gratitude (flower, crystal, or water) to the Earth.

A Mini-Activation Ritual: Mary Magdalene - The Rose Priestess of Ascension

- Sit quietly with hands over your heart and womb or lower belly (one hand each).
- Call in the energy of Mary Magdalene to surround your aura.
- Inhale deeply, and on the exhale, speak out loud three times.
- *I AM open and ready to serve the Kingdom of Love and Light for the highest good of all.*
- Meditate on the Rose Frequency (visualizing pink roses opening in your heart).
- Work with Rose Quartz and Pink Lotus oils to amplify divine feminine love.
- Visualize pink roses with golden tips opening in your heart and womb or lower belly. These roses are connected by a golden infinity symbol aligned with your intention to create through service with love and Light.
- Feel your sacred heart and holy womb aligned by a golden infinity symbol.

- Whisper: "As Above, So Within. I embrace the sacred devotion to the path of divine service and unconditional love in all my creations on the New Earth Star."

How this prayer supports your Soul alignment and activation codes for ascension.

- You are anchoring into your golden infinity wave love connection between Divine Mother Cosmic Womb and Earth Mother Sophia Womb connecting with your heart-womb/hara.
- Opening your inner Heart-Womb Stargate and direct connection into the Celestial gateway and Divine Mother Sophia.
- You are creating deep remembrance of your original Divine Mother gateway through the dissolution of synthetic DNA and inverted pathways.
- You create a balanced, centering, and grounded connection between New Heaven and New Earth.
- You are creating your "bridge of Light" between Heaven & New Earth, anchoring into your expanded 12D chakra system.
- Entrains your ascension column of your "I AM" Angelic Soul Light by grounding you between Heaven And New Earth Star reality.
- You open your multidimensional levels of consciousness to directly root yourself into the New Earth Star 5th to 7th-dimensional reality.

- Activates the Magdalene Womb codes and returns to the Holy Grail, the Womb of Sophia.
- Dissolving deeply held emotions and matrix programming blocking your Womb or Hara.

Heart Reflections And Journal Prompts

- What vision is my Soul asking me to serve from the higher realms, and how can I ground it in daily life?
- Where am I still divided between Heaven and Earth, and how can I become the union?
- What does proper *safety in embodiment* feel like in my physical body? Where do I resist it?

A Prayer Message And Activation with Archangel Metatron

The purpose of this prayer is holy, the union between body and soul, integration of the heaven plane, immersed within the earth plane, particles of pure love, the Light become the dominant vibration, bringing unity and peace into your body and Soul, intertwined with the divine source, creator and complete union. This prayer creates the internal structures to hold the pure frequencies of your Soul. It is the foundation for the sacred union of inner Heaven to outer Earth or matter. The formless flow into the form. Particles of love replace the previous condition, particles of experiences that hold the beliefs, judgments, imprinting, and conditioning of Separation from the Source. This is a falsehood, a lie you have adopted as untrue, creating an internal illusion within you.

The Soul medicine key is the feeling of knowing, feeling, seeing, hearing, being fully present, and being open to the true expression of myself to come into my experience now. This is the state of Heaven and Earth and divine union with my Soul. No doubt exists now as you are anchored in complete trust and faith in this state of knowing.

I am fully connected to my internal, authentic self, divine spark, and Soul Light; I am sealing this truth into my body and being with these words and frequencies of pure love, God's particles of primordial creation.

These God particles are not stagnant, but always moving, fluid and flexible waves washing in and out of time-space of physical matter, worlds as you focus on this prayer, it is a manifestation of your higher desire to connect fully with your Angelic Soul nature and individuated divine spark into form. This prayer is the divine bridge of Heaven to heart and Soul, embodied in form. A mirror image of Heaven is projected into your physical form of matter; your physical body and vessel become *illuminated* with pure love, Light, particles, and reflections of your angelic Soul, your perfected state of wholeness, shines brightly as a mirror of you, of your Soul, shimmering through your aura and Light body,

A seal of Divine perfection encases every particle and wave. The flow of wholeness within you, a divine tribulation and orchestration in motion beyond time and space, unites within your physical manifestation of holy union. This is the sacred union within your Angelic Soul, the Light of divinity married into your avatar body. Heaven is both yin and yang manifested as divine perfection in form, your body as a sacred temple and vessel. Your body is an elemental being and is your physical avatar. A divine creation is birthed.

Channeled on April 13, 2024, with the Angels and Archangel Metatron.

PRAYER ONE

HEAVEN ON EARTH: ANCHORING THE NEW EARTH STAR

*"A Grounding Prayer To Anchor
The Magdalene Frequency"*

*I connect my physical body and vessel
deep into the arms of Mother Earth
allowing her to hold me safely and gently,
I feel fully secure inside her loving womb.
I open my own Consciousness fully and enter through the
Stargate Of time to connect with the highest heavens of the
cosmos that they lift me up to my Divine connection with All
That Is. I AM connected to Heaven and Earth.
As Above So Below. As Within So Without.
I AM open and ready to serve the Kingdom of Love and Light
For the highest good of All.
So Be It, and So It Is! It is Done!*

ASCENSION PRAYER GATEWAY TWO

THE DESCENT OF THE DIVINE FLAME

"A Prayer of Higher Self Embodiment"
Metatron's Cube

Ascension Key Codes: Divine Union · Higher Self · I AM Presence · Atman (Divine Spark)

The Prayer Medicine

This luminous prayer evokes a sacred alignment between the Soul, path, and inner sovereignty. It is a powerful invocation of divine union, aligning your being with your Higher Self, the I AM Presence, and the Atman (Divine Spark). This prayer is a direct initiation into divine sovereignty, allowing you to shift from a fragmented self into a fully integrated light-being. It serves as a spiritual key to ascension, aligning you with New

Earth Star consciousness and the cosmic frequencies of Shekinah-Sophia, Metatron, and Christed Light.

This prayer invokes deep Goddess energies that align with higher self embodiment, divine sovereignty, and the merging of spirit and form. It activates Divine Feminine frequencies and calls in Divine Masculine energies, creating a sacred balance of unity between both aspects of the Soul. Metatron's Cube, a sacred geometric symbol, holds the blueprint for this integration and alignment with the I AM Presence.

It is a profound call to unify the ego self with the higher self, anchor divinity into the body, and live as the embodied I AM. This sacred act of inner merging aligns with three primary angelic rays, each serving as a dimension of the Soul's descent and embodiment. They form the inner halo through which your higher self gently merges with your human expression.

Your Over Lighting Divine Feminine - Masculine - Angelic Guides:

Call on these divine guides while invoking this prayer to support your pathway of Soul ascension every step of the way. They represent part of your Angelic Over-soul team guiding you home to a full reunion with your true Cosmic parents and "I AM" Angelic Soul.

Shekinah-Sophia Archetype includes Sophia/Cosmic Mother, Isis, Hathor, Lady Nada, and Mary Magdalene.

Metatron Archetype includes Metatron, Yeshua (Christ Consciousness), Archangel Michael, and Melchizedek.

Divine Feminine Archetype: Shekinah-Sophia

Shekinah-Sophia is the hallowed presence that does not arrive from above but emerges from within as you allow. She heals through stillness, not striving. She teaches through remembrance, not doctrine. She is the voice you hear in your Soul's quiet hour, whispering, *"I never left you. I dwell where you are willing to see Me."* Her essence is The *indwelling Spirit of God.* She who dwells within your breath, body, and heart. This prayer inspires you to embrace her feminine quality of holding the chalice of inner surrender that allows the ego to rest and divine presence to rise.

Divine Masculine Archetype: Metatron

Metatron oversees ascension, higher-dimensional access, and the full embodiment of divine sovereignty. He offers clarity, vertical alignment, and Soul sovereignty to fully anchor the higher self. His essence is "the eternal spark of divine intelligence, the Self that remembers you into Being." Metatron's Cube, a sacred geometric symbol, holds the blueprint for this integration and alignment with the I AM Presence.

How These Goddess Energies Work in This Prayer

The merging of the higher self with the physical self is an alchemical process of divine feminine wisdom. The Goddess energies activate the Light body, open the heart, and expand divine sovereignty within you. This is an initiation prayer. It brings a rebirth of spiritual awareness as the ego shifts to its rightful place beside the divine self rather than leading the journey.

Divine Union and The Sacred Balance of Masculine & Feminine

This prayer is a sacred marriage of Divine Masculine & Divine Feminine energies.

The role of the Divine Feminine or Goddess frequencies assists in receptivity, surrender, and heart activation. The Divine Masculine or God frequencies provide structure, protection, and clear spiritual will. When they are brought together, they harmonize into unity consciousness, allowing the Soul to fully enter its ascended divine state. Together, the sacred feminine and masculine become the One Presence you call into being: *"I AM."*

Angelic Rays: Together, these rays create the Trinity of Embodied Divinity

White Ray of Divine Illumination - Archangel Gabriel - brings the *"trumpet of remembrance,"* calling the Soul into holy alignment with the Source. He represents purity, Soul clarity, higher truth, and Soul communication. This prayer supports you in clearing egoic confusion and welcoming divine presence.

Pink Ray of Divine Love—Archangel Chamuel—allows the divine to *merge gently*, through love, not force. She represents unconditional love, self-worth, and Soul compassion. She inspires the heart-based alignment needed to receive one's true self.

The Gold Ray of Christed Wisdom—Archangel Uriel—illuminates the inner throne of your I AM presence. He represents illumined wisdom, peace, and Soul sovereignty. He supports you by grounding divine intelligence into embodied action.

How to Use This Prayer for Activation

- Speak it Aloud Daily: Your voice vibrates the codes into reality.
- Meditate on It. Visualize golden Light descending into your body as you merge with your Higher Self.
- Use It for Gridwork. Speak it over sacred sites to anchor divine frequencies into the planetary grid.
- Write It in Your Sacred Space. Place it on your altar to amplify its energy.

Mini-Activation: "I AM the Flame, I AM the Form"

- Sit comfortably, hands over heart and solar plexus.
- Breathe deeply and repeat silently or out loud:
  "Higher Self, merge now. Ego self, you may rest. I AM the Presence made whole."
- Visualize a rose-diamond flame descending from above and rising from below, meeting at your heart.
- Allow it to spiral gently through your spine, mind, body, and Soul, unifying you as one luminous self.

- Sit in silence, *feeling the merge* not as a concept but *as a living presence*.

How this prayer supports your Soul alignment and activation codes for ascension.

- Clears distortions from your energy field and creates an open channel to your Higher Self.
- When spoken aloud, it activates the Crown Chakra and Light Body Field.
- Harmonizes the Solar Plexus Chakra, allowing the Divine Will to take precedence over the personal will.
- Aligns you with your I AM Presence and Higher Self
- Activates the Divine Spark (Atman) within you.
- Creates an energetic bridge between spirit and matter.
- Harmonizes the Ego Self, making it a divine servant of the Higher Self.
- Triggers Hieros Gamos (Sacred Union) within your Light Body and lower four energy bodies.
- Anchors New Earth Consciousness and Metatronic Light Codes
- This is a divine Decree of Protection stating that you are held by higher forces, safe in your Soul's journey
- You empower yourself to fully activate your Avatar Light mastery, wisdom, and divine Soul truth.
- You are giving full permission for your Higher Self to become the leader of your Fifth-dimensional reality.
- You increase your capacity for ascension and your ability to access spiritual power.

Heart Reflections And Journal Prompts

- Where do I still believe I must "become" divine instead of remembering I already AM?
- What does my Higher Self truly want to express through me today in voice, action, or silence?
- How can I honor my ego not as an enemy but as a companion ready to serve the Light?

A Channeled Prayer Message From Mary Magdalene

Your Holy womb chakra (Hara) is the anchoring point for your Higher Self-connection within your body. It is the I AM, the Creator and the Source of your deepest knowing and truth. Just below the surface of your consciousness, place of birth and creation. It sits two fingers above the pelvic bone in the body's center. It coincides with the Sacral Chakra. Your womb center is where you hold your sovereignty, the space where you are sovereign and define your truth, reality, and power. The more you occupy this sacred space of your true Soul essence, the more aligned you are with your Higher Self. As you focus on expanding your Womb Light, you clearly and powerfully own your energy space. The voice in your womb is your Higher Self. *I AM Mary Magdalene*

A Channeled Prayer Message From Archangel Michael

You can invite peace into your life when you feel safe and protected. Release all negative energies in your life, let go, and let God handle these situations. Pray for guidance to lead you to a path of higher Light to fill your life now. ASK and receive it. Have faith and open your eyes to see your inner Light first. Focus on your inner Light and let it guide you through the darkness. As you focus on your inner Light, it grows in your life. Release all focus on the darkness; it does not serve you anymore. Your path is filled with the golden Light of peace, joy, and happiness. Place your focus here. *I AM Archangel Michael*

PRAYER TWO

THE DESCENT OF THE DIVINE FLAME

"A Prayer of Higher Self Embodiment"

Oh, Higher Self, Higher Self
come into Me now
connect with Me,
my I AM Divine Self,
My Atman Divine spark
I fully connect to Thee.
I gently move my Ego self to beside me now
and I ask for my Higher Self
to fully merge with
my mind, body, and Soul into
One presence now.
So Be It, and So It Is! It Is Done!

ASCENSION PRAYER GATEWAY THREE

ANCHORING DIVINE HEART LIGHT

"Anchoring Divine Light Through the Heart of Sovereignty"
The Rose Spiral

Ascension Key Codes: Christed Heart Light - Path of Illumination - Soul Alignment - Eternal Self

The Prayer Medicine

As you follow your expanding heart Light on your spiritual path, it leads you home, back to your Angelic Self-reflection. Your heart Light grows as you focus on holding and becoming your Soul Light. It shines brightly onto your pathway home through the darkness. I fear not, for all is well within and around me. The material world is a projection of your thought, creating worlds of form through imagination, worlds of form, and the illusionary cycles of time. You are Light in your truest form.

This prayer is a proclamation of unwavering Soul Light, representing spiritual courage, divine guidance, and the radiant expansion of heart-centered consciousness. The lines reflect a deep knowing of divine presence, trust in the path of Light, and surrender to the Soul's eternal essence. It is a robust heart-centered activation radiating divine Light, Soul alignment, and fearless embodiment of your true self.

The heart's radiant glow is the torch of ascension, illuminating the way forward, even in the depths of the spiritual night (transformation, ego dissolution, or the unknown). This prayer carries Divine Feminine and Divine Masculine energies, creating a harmonious balance between surrender and divine action. This prayer is a radiant expression of heart-light awakening, *spiritual courage*, and the deep alignment of the Soul with Light in shadowed places. It speaks of the *journey inward*, the *stability of love*, and the sacred act of bowing to the Eternal Self.

Your Over Lighting Divine Feminine - Masculine - Angelic Guides:

Call on these divine guides while invoking this prayer to support your pathway of Soul ascension every step of the way. They represent part of your Angelic Over-soul team guiding you home to a full reunion with your true Cosmic parents and "I AM" Angelic Soul.

Lady Mary Archetype includes: Lady Nada, Mary Magdalene, Mother Mary, and Quan Yin.

Metatron's Archetype includes: Archangel Michael, Thoth, and Archangel Uriel.

Divine Feminine Archetype: Lady Mary - Unwavering Rose Flame of the Heart

Lady Mary represents divine affirmation, spiritual steadiness, and trust in the inner flame. She brings inner peace through courage, devotion without self-denial, and light-bearing in darkened spaces. She also encourages compassionate radiance without ego attachment. Her symbol is the Unwavering Rose Flame of the Heart.

Divine Masculine Archetype: Archangel Michael – Sword of Soul Radiance

Archangel Michael protects the Soul's passage through fear and guides you into inner sovereignty. He stands at your side as you walk *"into the night"* as the guardian of your sacred flame, keeping it upright and fierce. He is the forthright Light that helps you claim: *"You are the Light, can't you see?"*

How These Goddess Energies Support You in This Prayer

This prayer is a radiant invocation of unwavering heart, Light, Soul courage, and divine remembrance, calling forth a symphony of feminine archetypes who walk you through the sacred night of transformation. Lady Mary anchors your inner radiance as the

Flame of Heart Illumination, steady and sovereign. Mary Magdalene walks beside your Soul in shadow, guiding you toward Light without fear. Lady Nada enfolds you in peace, dissolving fear with gentle devotion, while Mother Mary (Sophia-Mari) receives your sacred bow in grace, reminding you that surrender is strength. Together, these goddesses form a rose-coded field of empowerment and inner union, awakening your heart as both torch and temple on the path of the Highest Self-embodiment.

How The Divine Feminine and Masculine Energies Support You in This Prayer

The Divine Feminine and Masculine energies come together in a sacred dance of inner union, each playing a vital role in your Soul's embodiment. The Divine Feminine, through the presence of Lady Mary, Magdalene, Nada, and Mother Mary, offers the heart's unwavering flame, the embrace of compassion, and the soft strength of surrender, guiding your Soul with grace as it walks through shadow and into Light. She holds, nurtures, and reminds you of your inner holiness. Meanwhile, through archetypes like Michael and Enoch, the Divine Masculine provides spiritual clarity, courage, and alignment with divine will, empowering you to stand forthright in truth and claim your I AM presence. Together, they merge within your words and intention: the Feminine opens the heart, the Masculine affirms the Light, and in that union, you become the living flame of the Soul.

How to Use This Prayer for Personal Activation

- Speak it Aloud as a Morning Invocation will set your energy for the day.
- Call in your overlighting Divine Feminine - Masculine - Angelic Guides (see list above) by saying out loud:
- I call in the energies of Lady Mary, Lady Nada, Mary Magdalene, Mother Mary, and Quan Yin to surround me.
- I call in the energies of Archangel Michael, Thoth, and Archangel Uriel to surround me.
- Speak the prayer out loud three times while placing one hand on your Heart and the other on your Womb/lower belly, grounding the Light flow from "heaven to earth."
- Visualize your heart expanding into a deep ruby-red rose with golden waves radiating out the feeling of profound courage. Whisper: "I am the spiritual walker who embraces light and shadow equally. My heart awakens through the transforming ruby-golden flame, steady in the darkness."
- Write It in Your Sacred Space – Place it on your altar to amplify its frequency.

Mini-Activation: "Heart of Radiance"

- Sit or stand in quiet presence with hands over your heart.

- Visualize a ruby-golden flame expanding in your chest, glowing brighter with each breath.
- Speak out loud: "My heart is the lamp that does not waiver. It glows through night and sings of dawn."
- I am the radiant one who walks in love."
- Feel the Light pulse beyond your body, becoming a halo of golden Soul radiance.
- Let your body become the ruby-golden flame of the night, steady and sacred.

How this prayer supports your Soul alignment and activation codes for ascension.

- You are invoking the energies of Archangel Michael to help you feel a release from fear and detachment from worldly concerns. You are invoking the energies of protection, courage, truth, and strength.
- You are asking to experience a life of more joyfulness, access to your higher Truth, revealing hidden knowledge, and helping you to realize your full potential.
- Activate and heal your throat chakra as the power center and your divine will center.
- To help you invoke the energy of Faith so you can trust life more, which unlocks the flow, ease, and abundance of life.
- Release any remaining density of trauma held in the physical body to clear and dissolve from your cellular memory

- Teach you how to protect and shield yourself and the courage to stand on your own two feet
- You become the "peaceful warrior" and slay your demons and your own shadows.
- You release "fear" to fully embody your True Self and maintain sacred boundaries.
- Live beyond fear and illusion, standing as a pillar of Light and Truth.
- Help you remove negative energies.
- Achieve psychic protection.
- Speak your truth with kindness and honesty.

Heart Reflections and Journal Prompts

- What parts of myself do I still hide from my own Light?
- What does "walking into the night with my soul" mean for me now?
- When I fully bow to my true self, what am I surrendering—and what am I claiming?

A Prayer Meditation with Mother Mary

The Rose of your heart is opening now to receive its guidance, to direct your path in all ways into new Light and realms of celestial fields of bliss and joy you have not experienced before in human form; your angelic wings are opening and ready to take flight in new ways of living and being as an Ascended Earth Angel. Your journey is complete, lessons learned well; your Soul is ready to soar into the diamond Light. Hold yourself lightly and allow the goddess to emerge from within you now; take flight into the arms of the unknown world you seek. Have no fear. You are already there. Your heart knows the way home, beloved child. Have faith in yourself. You cannot get it wrong. Follow my lead and take my hand. Your Soul awaits. Close your eyes, come into your heart, and meet me here on the inner planes of Light in the temple of your rose heart, where peace and love prevail. A softness surrounds you, the sweetness of the mother enfolds you, and a wave of love deepens you. Open your heart now to receive this new sweet embrace. Feel the resonance of the solar Christ Consciousness wave flowing through your energy, through every cell, molecule, and particle; open your divine mind and see the Light of God, particles flowing in, receive the manna of Heaven's Grace raining down inside you of a new embrace, new sensations of joy, flowing in every direction, lifting you into a new realm of creation, of divine perfection. Release the past. Let go and let in your new world of joy and bliss.

Breathe through your heart, move deep into the tunnel of Light, and walk with me into the Light of Heaven. The New Earth awaits your conscious connection. Just say yes to open her heart and align with her. Stand still and receive your initiation of Heaven's Light. Pause and open the veil of angelic Light. See and feel these rays emitting now from your heart, hands, feet, and chakras. Embrace this angelic Light of yours, dear one; allow it in. Have no fear; let it be, let it be! Now and forevermore, you are the Light, can you see? Let it in, let it in. See a white vortex of Light spinning around your body and being as you become illuminated. *I AM Mother Mary*

Channeled Message From Mother Mary

I am at peace with my life in this present moment, the chaos, the transformation, the death of what is. I am at peace with everything. I drop all resistance to my path of reunification with my true self. I trust in the divine plan of the Goddess to transcend my inner world, bringing transformation to unite my threefold flame of unification with the divine. I am at peace with the truth that I exist beyond this body and world of form, and I am okay with this. I am at peace. I am the Way, the Truth, and the Light of God, Goddess. *I AM Mother Mary*

PRAYER THREE

ANCHORING DIVINE HEART LIGHT

"Anchoring Divine Light Through the Heart of Sovereignty"

Expanding heart Light glows deep inside of Me.
It waivers not for all to see
It guides my path into more Light
As I walk with my Soul into the night
I fear not, for all is well within and around me.
You are the Light, can't you see?
Stand forthright and let it be
Forever Me, I bow to Thee
So Be It, and So It Is! It is Done!

ASCENSION PRAYER GATEWAY FOUR

THE VOW OF SOUL LIGHT

"Anchoring The Divine Light of Service and Sovereignty"
The Six-Pointed Star

Ascension Key Codes: **Hieros Gamos (Sacred Union) - Divine Sovereignty - Full Divine Embodiment**

The Prayer Medicine

In this prayer, Quan Yin encourages you to awaken your sovereign divinity, embrace your true identities, and activate your full potential. She emphasizes the return of the Great Mother's love, urging you to open your heart-light and higher mind to receive her grace. Quan Yin guides you to your new home through the Cosmos and encourages you to walk boldly towards your divine destiny, embracing your angelic self and achieving eternal freedom.

This prayer declares divine service, sovereignty, and Soul embodiment. It pulses with the energy of Soul mission, Light anchoring, and the reclamation of sacred identity. This is a prayer and a *Soul contract spoken aloud*, awakening the deeper architecture of your I AM presence.

This prayer carries profound frequency and spiritual charge, a robust activation of Divine Sovereignty, service to the Light, and soul-path alignment. It is not just for personal sovereignty but for planetary ascension; it activates your mission and contributes to the collective awakening. It holds an 11:11 key, a spiritual password that connects you to your divine blueprint and is a divine decree. Use this prayer to build real change in the physical world.

The Vow of Soul Light honors the sacred Soul contract and the merging of remembrance, devotion, and the active embodiment of your Higher Self. It is a living vow encoded into your being and anchoring you into the New Earth as an act of service. With every invocation, you fully embody your celestial sovereignty and anchor the Light of the New Earth Star. Use this prayer to complete your karmic cycles and fully enter your Soul mastery timeline.

It is more than a prayer and a powerful decree of divine sovereignty, fully activating the I AM Presence and sacred union with your Soul Light. It carries the energy of divine inheritance, self-realization, and full embodiment of divine power. You are not just making a request but a proclamation giving a command to activate your sovereign divinity, holy Light, and sacred union with the higher self.

Your Over Lighting Divine Feminine - Masculine - Angelic Guides:

Call on these divine guides while invoking this prayer to support your pathway of Soul ascension every step of the way. They represent part of your Angelic Over-soul team guiding you home to a full reunion with your true Cosmic parents and "I AM" Angelic Soul.

Sophia-Isis Archetype: includes Isis, Sophia, Shekinah, Mary Magdalene and Quan Yin

Metatron Archetype includes: Metatron, Archangel Uriel, Archangel Sandalphon, St. Germain

Divine Feminine Archetype: Sophia-Isis - Emerald Heart Flame

Sophia-Isis represents wisdom in action, divine remembrance, and Soul sovereignty. She activates your role as a Priestess or Priest of Light, aligning cosmic identity with earthly service. She brings the gifts of Guardian of Divine Truth and reclamation of the Light body. Her symbol is the Emerald Heart Flame, which represents divine service through the heart and the merging of truth (emerald) and divine action (gold). This involves Elemental Energy, the Earth-Cosmic Bridge anchoring star codes into Earth Mother crystalline heart-womb grid.

Quan Yin - Goddess of Compassion, Mercy, and Grace

Goddess Quan Yin is associated with the 5th Ray or Green Ray of Healing and Consecration, and sometimes with the Pink Ray of Unconditional Love and Compassion. Her vibrational qualities are soft, flowing, receptive, and nurturing. She supports your ascension pathway with emotional healing, forgiveness, gentleness, and the merciful path to enlightenment.

Divine Masculine Archetype: Metatron - Golden Flame of Sovereign Service

Metatron represents divine order, higher will, and divine timing. He stabilizes your intention to walk purposefully, grounding your I AM alignment into action. He activates the Golden Flame of Sovereign Service, ensuring your destiny is soul-led.

This prayer connects to Ascended Master St. Germain and The Violet Flame.

Ascended Master St. Germain is the Keeper of the Seventh Ray and The Violet Flame. His role as Alchemist of the I AM Flame supports you with divine service, Light anchoring and planetary mission, spiritual sovereignty, and alchemical transformation of karmic patterns. The Violet Flame is a transmuting spiritual fire that clears, purifies, and elevates all not aligned with the Soul's divine truth. The key function of the Violet Flame is to transmute density into Light and seed the

Earth with heavenly radiance. It works cellularly, transmuting ancestral memory and igniting Soul codes stored in the body.

How to Use This Prayer for Activation

- Speak it out loud as a Morning Invocation.
- Speak it, standing tall, feeling the full energy of divine service filling you.
- Call in your over-lighting Divine Guides (see list above) by saying out loud:
- I call in the energies of Isis, Sophia, Shekinah, Mary Magdalene, and Quan Yin to embrace me.
- I call in the energies of Metatron, Archangel Uriel, Archangel Sandalphon, and St Germain to embrace me.
- Speak the prayer out loud three times while placing one hand on your Solar Plexus (power) and Heart (love) and the other hand on your Crown (divine connection) while speaking each phrase.
- Visualize emerald-gold rose Light expanding from your core, anchoring into Earth Mother's crystalline heart-womb emerald core. Activating divine service through the heart, the merging of truth (emerald) and divine action (gold)
- Write It in Your Sacred Space. Place it on your altar of love to remind you of your divine mission.

Mini-Activation: "I AM the Anchor of Light"

1. Stand upright (barefoot if possible), spine straight but not rigid.
2. Place your left hand over your heart and right over your solar plexus.
3. Inhale deeply and speak aloud: "I reclaim my Light, my Love, my Faith. I walk as the torch of the Divine."
4. Visualize an emerald-gold pillar of Light descending from the Central Sun, entering your crown, spiraling down to your feet, and then into the Earth's crystalline heart.
5. Inhale deeply and speak out loud: I AM the earth-cosmic bridge of truth and divine action. I AM the Flame, and I walk the Path. So be it. So it is. It is done.
6. Remain still for several breaths, feeling your cells receive divine Light.

How this prayer supports your Soul alignment and activation codes for ascension.

- You are reclaiming your complete faith, confidence, and trust that opens the door to your Divine God Self.
- You are anchoring your full flow of love and Light to enter the moment and your human vessel.
- You are invoking the remembrance of your original

contract with the Divine Creator to anchor the Light of your Soul into New Earth.
- You are anchoring the new frequencies of Light through your body into Mother Earth - Christ Consciousness grid.
- You are choosing, of your own free will, to return fully to the Light of our original source of life, the Cosmic Womb of Mother Divine.
- You are fully reinstating and restoring your Soul Light Bodies' original condition and perfection.
- You are fully reclaiming your Divine God Self-connection. As divine sovereign beings, we do this based on our divine authority.
- Invoke the power of the Violet Flame of Transmutation to restore your God qualities of freedom, transmutation, and transformation.
- You are invoking the Light of God particles to infuse and activate your 12-strand DNA
- You are invoking your immortal True Christed Self into physical form.

Heart Reflections and Journal Prompts

- What does it mean for me to *truly* serve the Light today not in ideal but in action?
- Where in my body do I still hold doubt or separation from my Divine God Self?

- If my Soul wrote a vow into my bones, what sacred sentence would it say aloud to the world?

Channeled Message From Higher Dimensions - Goddess Quan Yin

Call upon me now to activate your sovereign divinity, your truth, your real identity, your Angelic goddess self, and release your mask of sorrow and mundaneness. Wake up to the Light of your Soul; your true, radiant nature calls you home. Activate your full potential. Now, there is no reason to wait. You do not need permission to rise. And that's RISE! I am Quan Yin. I lived among your people many moons ago. I know the hardship and suffering you endure, which is now coming to an end; the great mother's love returns to embrace you in a robe of shimmering Light that warms your heart and deepens your breath into the fullness of life, awakens your mind to hear her call. She beckons you into her great stillness and ocean of love. Open your arms wide to receive her grace that falls upon your humanness like the Stardust of your mother's milk; it feeds your celestial Soul with her loving grace. Embrace me now, a child of the universe; my blood is your blood. My heart is your heart. My Soul is your Soul. Our hearts beat as one unified Soul. Can you feel it? Can you hear it? The waves crashing upon your shores, the ebb and flow of the mother's heart flows within your every cell, your quantum Light, your cosmic Soul Mirror, mirror on the wall. Who's the brightest of them all? You are! Blinded by your Light. O, radiant Soul.

Your diamond heart shines forth, transforming the darkness to become one unified Light.

Walk beside me now, and I will show you the way home as your Light-body undergoes a Chrysalis transformation extraordinaire, your new home awaits like a Tiny Dancer. You make your way across the stars, spreading your Light along the way, illuminating your Angelic self's great potential into the Light of a new dawn unfolding. Golden Child of the universe, rise and take your seat on the throne of your divine mystery. A great unveiling awaits you, dear one; it is time to see your true Angelic Self, unravel your deepest mystery, and embrace your divine wholeness. Rise and take my hand. I will show you the way. Don't look back. Keep your eyes forward on the new golden path of your destiny, walk bravely with conviction in your heart and peace in your mind, and may you be forever and eternally free to fly your way Through the Heaven's Gate, your beloved sister; *I AM Quan Yin*

PRAYER FOUR

THE VOW OF SOUL LIGHT

"Anchoring The Divine Light of Service and Sovereignty"

*In this moment, I reclaim all my faith,
all my love, and all my Light.
As a divine sovereign being and child of the cosmos.
I remain Steadfast in my duty to carry
the torch of Light for the Divine and
To anchor this Light into Mother Earth for the
highest good of All. This declaration of my true desire to serve
the Light and only The Light is written into every
cell of my body and being. I call forth my Divine God Self
connection now in this moment and Every moment to lead me
forward on the highest path of my Souls destiny that I
fully embrace with all my heart and Soul.
So Be It, and So It Is! It Is Done!*

ASCENSION PRAYER GATEWAY FIVE

PRAYER OF LIGHT FOR THE NEW EARTH ANGEL

"A Soul Declaration of Divine Radiance and Unity"
Rose Tree of Life

Ascension Key Codes: I AM Presence - infinite divine love - High Heart/Womb activation - Unity Consciousness

The Prayer Medicine

This prayer invites you to fully align with, merge with, and embody your Angelic Soul frequency and vibration of divine love and Light. To fully merge our light body and physical body temple with zero degrees of separation from our divine Soul. To fully dissolve all the false, illusionary, synthetic structures of the false God world held within your energy hologram. To release all quantum entanglements trapping your

Light into the world of illusion and matter. To fully reclaim your true eternal nature of divine love and bliss is your reunion with Heaven while living on Mother Earth.

This prayer is a soul-coded invitation to fully merge with your Angelic Higher Self and embody the eternal Light and love of your divine nature. It activates a complete union of your Light body and physical vessel, dissolving all false matrices, illusions, and quantum entanglements that obscure your truth. Rooted in the Universal Law of One, it affirms that you are already one with the Light of the Creator. It calls you to reclaim your whole Soul Light, anchor your I AM presence into the Womb of Divine Feminine flow, and awaken the Christos-Sophia Diamond Sun template within you. It is a wake-up call, radiant blessing, awakening remembrance, and dissolving separation.

A Soul transmission of divine remembrance, a radiant affirmation of unity with Source, and a call to embody the eternal Light within all beings. It is gentle yet potent, activating the profound truth that *you are not separate from the Light; you are its fragrance, form, and flame.* This prayer activates a transcendent affirmation of divine identity, unity, and Light embodiment. It flows like a soul-lit blessing, awakening remembrance, dissolving separation, and activating the radiant nature of the Eternal Self. This solar-angelic declaration invites the Soul to rise into its divine fragrance, power, and presence.

Your Over Lighting Divine Feminine - Masculine - Angelic Guides:

Call on these divine guides while invoking this prayer to support your pathway of Soul ascension every step of the way. They represent part of your Angelic Over-soul team guiding you home to a full reunion with your true Cosmic parents and "I AM" Angelic Soul.

Lady Sophia Archetype includes: Sophia, Lady Nada, Mary Magdalene, and Mother Mary

Solar Logos Archetype includes: Cosmic Christ frequency, Archangel Uriel, Seraphim Choir

Divine Feminine Guides Lady Sophia – The Luminous Rose Heart

Lady Sophia is a high-frequency divine feminine archetype, an emanation of the Sophianic Flame united with the Essence of Divine Love. She is not a historical figure but a multi-dimensional presence revealed through Soul gnosis, rose path initiations, and sacred remembrance. She carries the vibration of wisdom (Sophia) fused with love and guides souls ready to awaken, soften, and embody their Light in graceful sovereignty. She brings in the soft radiance of truth that dissolves all fear of separation and reminds the Soul that it has never been separated.

Divine Masculine: Solar Logos - The Radiant Sun Self

The Solar Logos includes divine masculine forces that activate the I AM flame within you, encouraging embodiment, clarity, and expansion. They do not dominate; they ignite within. The eternal I AM flame of divine presence is the masculine sun ray that gives life and structure to all. He brings the commanding Light of unity and the frequency that activates truth in concept and Soul embodiment. He illuminates the *sovereign Self* and calls it to rise with clarity, dignity, and purpose.

How to Use This Prayer for Activation

Speak It As a Light Decree (Daily I AM Alignment)

Purpose: To anchor your I AM presence and Soul Truth

Aligns your body, voice, and field to your original divine identity and harmonizes your daily path with Source Light.

- Stand or sit in a posture of regal stillness.
- Place one hand on your Heart, one on your womb or lower belly.
- Call in your over-lighting Divine Guides (see list above) by saying out loud:
- I call in the energies of Sophia, Lady Nada, Mary Magdalene, and Quan Yin to embrace me.
- I call in the energies of Solar Logos, Cosmic Christ Frequency, Archangel Uriel, and St Germain to embrace me.
- Speak each line of the prayer with breath and intention.

- Pause between lines to *feel the energy of the words move through you.*
- Visualize yourself as an eternal Rose Tree of Light, fully rooted into the New Earth Star. With your arms moving upward toward the heavens, merging into Oneness, you become a tower of pure white celestial Light.
- End by saying three times: "I claim my Light. I walk as Light. I shine for All."

How to Activate the Codes of Divine Remembrance and Embody Your Eternal Rose Tree of Life

These codes already live within you. This prayer is the key that unlocks their flowering. To activate them consciously:

Pray with Full Presence: Breath + Word = Light Code Transmission

Speak your prayer aloud slowly, feeling each word as a vibration.

Breathe between each line to allow integration.

Hold your hand over your heart as you say: *"The fragrance of your own soul light..."* and visualize it awakening a solar rose-gold within your heart.

This breath-work practice acts as an activation, unfolding ancient memories from your Soul's library.

How to Embody Your Eternal Rose Tree of Life

Your Eternal Rose Tree of Life is the fusion of the Kabbalistic Tree and Soul Rose Mandala, the structure of your divine Light woven into a physical being. To embody it:

Womb (or Hara) and Heart Spiral Activation

- Place one hand on your womb or lower belly and one hand on your heart.
- Speak: *"Let it shine bright and brighter. Eternal bliss is yours in this Light.*
- Visualize a spiral of rose-gold Light connecting both centers, forming the trunk of your Soul tree.
- With each breath, the Light roots into Gaia and rises into the stars
- This anchors the divine architecture of your Rose Tree of Life into your physical and Light body.

Mini-Activation: "Fragrance of My Soul Light"

- Sit quietly with a rose (or visualize one) inside your heart and your womb or lower belly.
- Inhale deeply, breathing into your heart, and exhaling out your liquid love-light into your womb or lower belly.
- Speak out loud three times: "I AM the Light. I AM the Fragrance of Eternal Love."
- Visualize your Soul Light radiating outward like rose-gold petals filled with luminous scent, weaving gently

around your heart, womb, and body, creating an oval shape of pure love around you.
- Whisper: "My light is sweetness. My soul is bloom. My being is eternal."
- Feel yourself *opening like a cosmic rose* to receive and radiate love and Light everywhere.

How this prayer supports your Soul alignment and activation codes for ascension.

- Recenter in truth and unify your Soul parts by reclaiming all your Soul Light back into your body.
- You are invoking the Light of God particles to infuse with your multi-dimensional 12D Chakra system.
- This prayer is your "wake-up call." It is time to actively rejoin your true self and nature again, to fully activate the Christos-Sophia Diamond Sun Template within you.
- You are already One with the Light of the Creator and not separate from it.
- You must reclaim all of your Soul Light to rise, realize, and join with your eternal nature.
- Awakening into remembrance that Divine Love is your original eternal state, weaving all of life everywhere.
- Activating your Rose Tree of Life will allow you to develop higher spiritual awareness and build the Lightbody connection with your higher streams and vibrations of Soul, monad, and avatar consciousness.

- Activating Higher chakra 5D powers: magical, shamanic powers, Soul traveling, telekinesis or telepathy, communication with Ascended Masters, Archangels, and Galactic Star Beings.

Heart Reflections and Journal Prompts

- Where do I still believe I must *earn* the Light rather than *remember* that I am it?
- If my Soul had a fragrance, what would it feel like? How would it bless others?
- What is one way I can shine my Light *without apology* today—for the good of All?

A Prayer Message From Divine Mother Sophia

I am the Light. You are the Light. You are Light incarnate in a new world. Now, focus only on the Light of the source, not any external source. Your strength to hold your truth is in merging with your own Light. As you merge into greater expansion of your own Light, your consciousness changes, and you can move into higher dimensions of Light; you will feel Light as a feather as you ascend with your Light body. Your Merkabah vehicle that carries your Light body activates with each change in consciousness. It becomes more automatic and fluid without you trying to do anything. Your intention and desire to become your Ascended Angelic Soul Self are all required. This desire is activated by your Soul path predestined before your physical birth, an image of a sun. You are like the sun's rays coming out from your source, All That Is, Divine Mother-Father God. You are the sun, the moon, and the stars. You see, all of that is your beloved Soul. Blessed Be Divine Angel!

PRAYER FIVE

PRAYER OF LIGHT FOR THE NEW EARTH ANGEL

"A Soul Declaration of Divine Radiance and Unity"

I AM the Light of God You are the Light of God
All is eternal in the flow of Love
None can be lost or separated from this Light
You are One with the Light Embrace this truth in your heart
Open to receive more Light All is well within the Light
Your Light is needed now Shine forth your great Light
To honor All, embrace your Light
Your sweetness flows in this Light,
The fragrance of your own Soul Light
Let it shine bright and brighter
Eternal bliss is yours in this Light.
Claim it now and rise into eternity forever!
So Be It, and So It Is! It is Done!

ASCENSION PRAYER GATEWAY SIX

I AM THAT I AM

"A Declaration of Divine Inheritance"
Metatron's Cube

Ascension Key Codes: **Magdalene-Christic Key - Divine Inheritance - Sovereignty**

The Prayer Medicine

This is a solar decree of embodiment, where your Soul steps fully into its divine inheritance as a sovereign flame of love and Light. It is a temple invocation, activating sacred remembrance, radiant union, and the divine right to embody your Highest Self.

The Light of our souls and Source Creator God, All That Is. Upon stating these words to ourselves, we are signaling to our

Higher Self and "I AM" presence our return back to our source. Activating the Light codes within our DNA template, we move forward within the unique pathway of our individual ascent back into the Light of Source. Activating these Light codes brings in the new experiences, gifts, lessons, people, and places our Higher Self has planned for our next Soul evolution within this lifetime.

This living Light prayer is a Declaration of Divinity across all timelines. Through your words, you command the embodiment of your Soul's inheritance and Light service. This Magdalene-Christic Key activates your return to the Throne of Christ's Light.

Your Over Lighting Divine Feminine - Masculine - Angelic Guides:

Call on these divine guides while invoking this prayer to support your pathway of Soul ascension every step of the way. They represent part of your Angelic Over-soul team guiding you home to a full reunion with your true Cosmic parents and "I AM" Angelic Soul.

Queen Sophia Archetype includes: Sophia, Shekinah, Mother Mary, Isis, Mary Magdalene and Quan Yin

Enoch-Metatron Archetype includes: Enoch, Archangel Metatron

Angelic Energy: Archangel Sandalphon and Archangel Zadkiel

Divine Feminine Guide: Queen Sophia – Crowned Flame of Holy Feminine Sovereignty

Queen Sophia is a divine feminine archetype of profound radiance, sovereignty, and Soul embodiment. It emanates Sophia, the Primordial Wisdom Flame, fused with heavenly Light, clarity, or a luminous crown. Queen Sophia is the aspect of the Divine Mother who remembers, restores, and enthrones the Light within you. She appears as the Crowning Presence, anointing you with the remembrance that your divinity is not borrowed but *innate*. She calls you to claim your throne, not through Ego, but through sacred responsibility and Soul Light embodiment. She reminds you that divine inheritance is your birthright, and your holiness is *within you*, not outside or withheld.

Divine Masculine Guide: Enoch-Metatron - Pillar of Divine Authority

Enoch-Metatron is a Divine Masculine archetype of Light architecture, divine remembrance, and Soul embodiment, representing a multi-dimensional lineage of ascended mastery. He stands as a pillar of ascension, the scribe of God, and the Master of the Lightbody Temple, guiding souls into complete merger with their divine structure and Source blueprint. It is the Divine Masculine Current of Structure, Radiance, and Sovereign Memory. He builds the inner temple of the Soul in harmony with your Higher Self and anchors the will of the Source through sacred declaration. He is the guardian of your divine identity and the scribe of your Light destiny.

Angelic Energy Guide: Archangel Sandalphon and Archangel Zadkiel

Sandalphon grounds your divine authority into the Earth grid and brings prayers into physical reality.

Zadkiel clears blockages to divine memory and supports the phrase *"I claim all of thee"* as a complete merger with the Eternal Self.

How to Use This Prayer for Activation

Morning And Evening Decree:

- Speak it, standing tall, feeling the full energy of divine power flowing through you.

Chakra Activation Meditation:

- Place your hands on your Solar Plexus, Heart, and Crown while speaking each phrase.
- Visualize golden Light expanding from your center, filling your entire aura with divine sovereignty.

Manifestation And Gridwork:

- Speak this prayer over water or sacred objects to charge them with divine Light.
- Use it before energy healing, meditation, or planetary service work.

Write And Place It on Your Sacred Altar of Love: Let it be a daily reminder of your divine mastery.

Mini-Activation: "Crowning the I AM Flame"

- Stand or sit with a tall spine and feet on the earth.
- Place your hands on your crown and speak:
- *"I AM That I AM. I crown myself in divine remembrance. I claim all of thee."*
- Visualize a violet-gold flame descending from above your head, gently settling into your crown and radiating down your spine.
- Whisper: *"I am sovereign. I am divine. I am whole."*
- Let the flame seal around you like a golden mantle of authority and grace.

How this prayer supports your Soul alignment and activation codes for ascension.

- You are awakening your true divine power and "reclaiming it" back into your present moment.
- You are reclaiming your complete faith, confidence, and trust that opens the door to your Divine God Self.
- You are anchoring your full flow of love and Light to enter the moment and your human vessel.
- You are invoking the remembrance of your original contract with the Divine Creator to anchor the Light of your Soul into New Earth.

- You are anchoring the new frequencies of Light through your body into Mother Earth - Christ Consciousness grid.
- You are choosing, of your own free will, to return fully to the Light of our original source of life, the Cosmic Womb of Mother Divine.
- You are fully reinstating and restoring your Soul Light Bodies' original condition and perfection.
- You are fully reclaiming your Divine God Self-connection. As divine sovereign beings, we do this based on our divine authority.
- Invoke the power of the Violet Flame of Transmutation to restore your God qualities of freedom, transmutation, and transformation.
- You are invoking the Light of God particles to infuse and expand into your 12-strand DNA
- You are invoking your immortal True Christed Self into physical form.

Heart Reflections and Journal Prompts

- Where have I unconsciously denied or diminished my divine sovereignty?
- What would it mean for me to fully claim my spiritual inheritance in my daily life?
- What parts of myself are ready to merge back into my Soul Light now, without condition or delay?

A Channeled Healing Process From Mary Magdalene

When you have unloving thoughts about yourself or others, when a loving thought arises in your conscious awareness, this is a sign that you are ready to release it from your energy bodies permanently. It is important not to deny or repress this imperfect thought that is arising, for this is the way of purification of your Soul and mental body. Look at it and observe the thought from outside of yourself. See the thought on a blank movie screen in your mind. Now, take a golden eraser and wipe the screen clean, picking up all the residue so that only a blank white slate or white screen is left. Take a deep breath in and say, Go in peace, or all is well. You may say the word delete over the word or words and then say, Go in peace. These commands are given by you because you are taking full responsibility for your creations. You can use the visualization process or the audio word command; both work equally well, so it's a personal preference to choose. As you release these unloving words and phrases, you reclaim your power in your divine Light, and you stand in your own authentic spiritual power. You are choosing love for yourself and for others. You are changing every energy composition and becoming a master of your new life; taking responsibility for all your actions and even your thoughts takes an act of courage to acknowledge the hidden dust in your closets that have been buried deep within, waiting for you to open the doors with your choice to allow the Light to enter again. Rejoice when you have this awareness and give praise for your life moving into more peace and joy. *I AM Mary Magdalene.*

PRAYER SIX

I AM THAT I AM

"A Declaration of Divine Inheritance"

I AM That I AM, I AM That I AM, I AM That I AM
I AM a Sovereign divine being of Love and Light in my own right!
I fully claim my divine inheritance now as decreed
by Heaven above All my power is fully activated now.
I AM Holy of the Holies. Pure divine Light fills me now.
I embrace my divinity and merge with my Soul Light
becoming one with thee!
In truth no separation exists only thine Light can be!
Shine forth my great Light
I claim all of me!
I claim all of me!
I claim all of me!
So Be It, and So It Is! It Is Done!

ASCENSION PRAYER GATEWAY SEVEN

WINGS OF THE SACRED HEART

A Rose Invocation of Innocence, Light, and Divine Perception
Rose Mandala

Ascension Key Codes: Innocence Restoration - Sacred Heart Expansion - Soul Guidance Integration

The Prayer Medicine

This prayer walks the Rose Path of the Heart, the journey of returning to your original Soul essence through sacred witnessing. In the Magdalene lineage, this is the *opening of the Holy Rose Chamber* within the High Heart, the place of divine remembrance and gentle power.

The Magdalene-Essene essence of this prayer reminds us of where the sacred heart becomes a compass, and your Light becomes the path. The wings symbolize the return to Soul sovereignty through inner clarity, love, and guidance received in grace. The Essene tradition reflects the practice of Angel communion, where the initiate opens all senses, not only physical, but spiritual sight, hearing, and knowing, to receive guidance and walk in divine service.

The prayer ascension codes are *frequencies of divine remembrance that* open your heart, align your senses with the Light, and reestablish your original Soul flame within the Earth and the Cosmos. This prayer teaches you how to ask for guidance and transforms you into a vessel capable of receiving it.

This prayer reminds you that *your Light is your compass, your heart is your guide*, and *your Soul already remembers the way home.*

Your Over Lighting Divine Feminine - Masculine - Angelic Guides:

Call on these divine guides while invoking this prayer to support your pathway of Soul ascension every step of the way. They represent part of your Angelic Over-soul team guiding you home to a full reunion with your true Cosmic parents and "I AM" Angelic Soul.

Divine Feminine Archetype includes: Mother Anna, Lady Isis, Mary Magdalene and Mother Mary.

Divine Masculine Archetype includes: Yeshua - Christos Flame, Joseph of Arimathea, Metatron.

Angelic Energy: Archangel Gabriel and Archangel Haniel, Angel of the Sacred Heart

Divine Feminine Guide: Mother Anna - *Grandmother Flame of the Rose*

Mother Anna, also known as Saint Anne or Hannah, is honored across sacred traditions as the grandmother of Yeshua (Jesus) and the mother of the Virgin Mary (Sophia-Mari). In the Magdalene and Essene Mysteries, she is revered as a High Initiate of the Rose Lineage, Temple Mother, and Holy Womb Grail Codes carrier. She supports your embodiment and nurtures the path of spiritual innocence and divine trust. Her gift supports opening your inner child to safely return to the sacred heart.

Divine Masculine Guide: Yeshua - Christos Flame — *Embodied Logos, Solar King, Beloved of the Rose*

Yeshua or Jesus the Christ, Bearer of the Christos Flame. Beyond the traditional religious lens, Yeshua in the Magdalene, Essene, and Rose Lineage teachings is a Divine Masculine avatar, a Soul who fully embodied the Christos-Sophia Light, walking Earth as the Living Flame of Divine Union. The Christos Flame is the eternal solar essence of Source Light; the primordial consciousness of union flows from the center of the Great Central Sun and anchors into humanity through the willing heart. Yeshua became this flame, not just in Spirit but in embodied form.

Divine Masculine Guide: Joseph of Arimathea - Guardian of the Sacred Vessel

Joseph of Arimathea, a revered yet often veiled figure in sacred texts, emerges in the Magdalene and Essene mystery traditions as a man of great earthly stature and as a spiritual guardian, vessel bearer, and lineage protector. He is known as the Guardian of the Sacred Vessel, entrusted with the Holy Grail's physical and metaphysical aspects. He embodies the Sacred Protector archetype: not dominating but guarding the vessel of divine purpose. He shows how true masculine energy offers structure, safety, and sovereignty to the unfolding divine feminine.

How to Use This Prayer for Activation

Speak It Daily for Divine Alignment:

- Say this prayer out loud in the morning to awaken divine vision.
- Place a white, gold, and pink candle on your sacred altar of love.

Use It in Meditation:

- Visualize spreading your wings and taking flight, stepping fully into your divine path.

Write out this Prayer and Place It on Your Altar:

- Keep this as a daily reminder that you already are the Light.

Speak It Out loud three times Before Dreaming:

- This will open the Third Eye and allow divine messages in your dreams.

Mini-Activation: "Wings of the Sacred Heart"

Time: Morning or dusk

Tools: A white rose (or visualized), a candle, soft instrumental tones

- Sit with your heart open, palms up on your lap
- Close your eyes and speak out loud: "I walk forward into the Light of my being. I open the eyes and ears of my soul. I receive divine guidance now with ease and grace."
- Visualize a pair of luminous wings unfolding from your heart.
- Each feather is a divine frequency of your Soul's Light.
- Feel these wings *lift you* into gentle awareness, not of escape, but of return.
- Say: "I open my sacred heart for all to see. I hear, I know, I feel. So Be It. So It Is. It Is Done."

- Let the Light settle into your crown, heart, and root.

How this prayer supports your Soul alignment and activation codes for ascension.

- Affirms your Soul as Light and a cosmic child of Source
- Reorients the path inward to the sacred heart and intuitive knowing
- Opens your Soul senses: see, hear, feel, know
- Teaches you to ask and *receive* divine wisdom with openness
- Grounds the process through holy praise and vibrational alignment
- Develop Soul discipline—seeing, feeling, knowing, and hearing through angelic and Christic Light perception.
- Activates the Rose Priestess rite of holy receptivity, arms and heart open in full surrender.
- Guides and directs you to re-enter your true Soul frequency, born of Light and innocence.

Heart Reflections and Journal Prompts

- Where in my life am I ready to return to soul-level innocence and release distortion?

- What divine message or frequency is trying to reach me through my sacred senses what do I *hear*, *see*, or *feel* in the unseen?
- If my sacred heart had wings, what would I trust to carry me toward next?

A Forgiveness Healing Process with Quan Yin

Restore your purity of heart and childlike Innocense

Use this healing process when you need to release judgment or seek forgiveness and release any accompanying emotions of shame or guilt for yourself, others, a situation or an event coming up from the past or the present. First connect with the beautiful energies of Quan Yin, by inviting her to wrap you in her arms of compassion for every part of your beautiful existence. As you do, you begin to reflect on the situation that's coming up, that includes some energy of judgment, or perhaps an area where you cannot obtain forgiveness for yourself or others. Bring that situation to mind. Now begin to get in touch with the deep emotions that want to arise for healing and transformation. Now begin to breathe Quan Yin into your Soul, feel her deep waters of compassion begin to unfold your every fractal of your beingness allowing her energy of compassion to permeate your mind, body, heart and Soul. Now imagine yourself merging with her into the oneness of All That Is as you do, you begin to notice as a bright crystalline white-violet Light begins to enter opening up new doors of awakening to more Light within you as you acknowledge and open to receive her energy of compassion and mercy, you begin to receive these great blessings as they start to begin to come down, opening your crown chakra, your lotus flower begins to open as pure violet Light now flows down from the crown into your body and being you begin to soak up the transforming energy of forgiveness into every part of your body and life which has been blessed with pure love. You open and receive these streams of violet Light as it enters the halls of your physical body, it permeates into the very fiber of your beingness, on the levels of your mental, your emotional, your spiritual and physical bodies of Light now releasing all judgment and energies of unforgiveness, freeing your Soul of all tombs of imprisonment, you now begin to breathe in this energy of freedom as the doors to your Soul unlock streams of higher Light begin to pour through you, elevating your consciousness into new ways of perceiving and living as an Ascended being of Light. Now, you see yourself walking in a new state of compassion and love. Your elevated state brings deep healing and forgiveness for every facet of your Soul's existence, your Soul is now free from the imprisonment of judgment and non forgiveness. Shame and guilt can never trap you again as you gently release it all into the waters of deep compassion. Quan Yin sweeps you in her embrace of gentleness and strength, weaving deep happiness and joy into your Soul. Now return to the present moment. Your suffering is over, and your pain is gone. Your glory is ever present, like the sun shines on and you begin to whisper inside and hear the voice of freedom arising. I am free. I am free. I am free. *So be it. So It Is! It Is Done!*

PRAYER SEVEN

WINGS OF THE SACRED HEART

"A Rose Invocation of Innocence, Light, and Divine Perception"

*Walk forward into the Light of your being cosmic child of the Universe returning to the innocence of your Soul
allow your sacred heart to guide you now.
Your Light shines bright for you to see what you need to see, what you need to hear, what you need to know and what you need to feel. Spread your wings and take flight you are the Light. Open your sacred heart for
all to see what you need to hear, know and feel.
Ask for your divine guidance now to be revealed,
embrace it fully with arms open wide
you receive it into your Soul with ease and grace.
Give thanks and praise holy blessings to thee!
So Be It, and So It Is! It is Done!*

ASCENSION PRAYER GATEWAY EIGHT

EARTH ANGEL GRATITUDE PRAYER

"I AM Grateful for My Life as a Co-Creator"
The Chalice And The Blade

Ascension Key Codes: **Gratitude Frequency Code - Trinitized Light Code - Divine Will Code - Lightbody**

The Prayer Medicine

In the beautiful prayer you are acknowledging you are already a Divine Creator Being now claiming your perfected state of divine human beingness. You are already whole and complete via your blueprint that holds your divine qualities of pure love and Light. As you accept, remember and awaken this truth within every cell and molecule of your body purifying all that is "false" dissolves within you. You already contain the true trinity of "love, Light and creation" within your blueprint made in the image of Mother/Father God. As you embrace all parts of yourself, mental/emotional/physical/spiritual with love, respect and gratitude you awaken fully into the new octave of divine love or the quantum field without separation. You are now fully "awake and a fully conscious sentient being" living in the Unity field. You are activating all 12 strands of your DNA in your Light bodies. You have truly liberated yourself returning to your original state of purity, and innocence as the cosmic child.

This prayer, is a radiant pillar of ascension support it weaves together remembrance, purification, and divine union. It does not merely affirm truth it anchors you into the frequencies of Lightbody awakening, Soul integration, and embodied divinity. This prayer guides your ascension by realigning you with truth, restoring your full divine memory, and harmonizing your human and divine selves in the moment. You are not waiting for ascension you are *living it*, breath by breath. These Light codes do not float above you they live within you, awakened by your spoken word, breath, and intention. This prayer is not simply a message it is a living scroll that opens your Lightbody Temple from within.

In the Rose Path, the heart is the chalice, and gratitude is the water that fills it. It softens the armor of the Ego and allows the soul-light to bloom through humility and wonder. Gratitude is not weakness it is reverent power. It can help dissolve separation, realign distorted perceptions and invite the Higher Self to lead you forward even through chaos and change. The beautiful energy of Gratitude is one of the highest forms of prayer. Gratitude calibrates the Soul to the frequency of reception and divine reciprocity. It attunes your field to what is already holy, rather than what is lacking. In ascension, where old identities are shedding and the unknown often opens before us, gratitude becomes the *energetic anchor* that stabilizes the inner temple.

Your Over Lighting Divine Feminine - Masculine - Angelic Guides:

Call on these divine guides while invoking this prayer to support your pathway of Soul ascension every step of the way. They represent part of your Angelic Over-soul team guiding you home to full reunion with your true Cosmic parents, and "I AM" Angelic Soul.

Divine Feminine Guide: Mary Magdalene

Divine Masculine Guide: Yeshua - Christos Flame

Divine Feminine Guide: Mary Magdalene

Mary Magdalene holds the Rose Grail of inner alchemical fire and helps dissolve all that is false with love. She supports you with Soul alchemy, truth through love, radiant purification.

Divine Masculine Guide: Yeshua - Christos Flame

Yeshua activates the Trinitized Light within and embodies the Law of Love in form. He supports you reclaim the Living Word, embodiment of truth, and sacred surrender.

Angelic Guide: Archangel Raphael:

Archangel Raphael balances the emotional body and clears distortion through green-gold healing Light. He brings divine healing, inner heart truth, and Soul integration.

How to Use This Prayer for Activation

Morning and Evening Invocation:

- Speak it out loud or in your heart to align with divine truth.

Sacred Water or Crystal Charging:

- Speak this prayer over a cup of water or a crystal to infuse it with divine energy.

Meditation and Breathwork:

- Place your hands over your heart and solar plexus, breathe deeply, and visualize golden Light filling your body.

Write It and Place It on Your Sacred Altar of Love:

- Keep this prayer as a sacred text in your spiritual space

Mini Activation: Trinity Breath of Gratitude

Time: Morning or during your spiritual practice

Position: Seated with hands on heart and womb or lower belly

- Inhale and speak: "I AM Grateful."
- Hold the breath and say inwardly: "I AM Truth."
- Exhale and affirm: "I AM Whole."

Repeat 3 times.

Visualize golden-white Light pouring into your heart and spiraling outward into your body and aura.

Whisper: "All of life is within me. I receive it in reverent joy."

How this prayer supports your Soul alignment and activation codes for ascension.

- Reclaims your role as *active participant in creation*
- Realigns you to organic Source flow, beyond false matrices increasing your inner guidance, stillness and trust
- Clears karmic debris, shame, distortion, illusion
- Heals the emotional lightbody and heart grid
- Harmonizes all body layers through resonance with Universal Law
- Enhances discernment, clarity, and faith in the unseen
- Supports full embodiment of the Christos-Sophia Diamond Sun Body
- Dissolves ego resistance and the illusion of control
- Restores exiled Soul aspects (inner child, wounded templates, past selves)

Heart Reflections and Journal Prompts

- What does co-creation with my inner Source feel like in my body today?
- What "false" thought or belief am I ready to purify from my Soul with love?
- How can I live the Holy Trinity of Love, Light, and Creation in my daily life?

A Healing Prayer Message From Mother Mary

The channeled message with Mother Mary. Dear One, you're most blessed today to have this opportunity to be in a body here on the Earth's plane for many may not feel directly connected to this wondrous gift you have been given. Having a physical body is a rare opportunity the Divine Creator gives. Many souls would love to have this opportunity to be in your experience in this moment. To be given this gift of a body is a great responsibility, because you have free will to choose how you will use this gift. Will you honor your body's wisdom and knowledge it wants to share with you, or will you throw it away and discard its inner treasures? It is always your choice, dear one. However, let me share the great secrets your body holds for you. It's nature is true and will never lie to you under any condition. It holds the keys to your enlightenment to reflect the imbalances in your mental, emotional, physical and spiritual bodies. Your ability to bring balance and transformation to a higher transcended state of being is accelerated while in the physical plane of matter. Your Soul patterns are reflected in the physical. They are heightened through reflection of your relationships to all living persons, places, situations, and even your animal friends with your intention and focus upon these patterns of imbalances, in your thoughts, words, actions that might manifest into your physical reality. You have the immediate opportunity to correct them and choose healthy creations for yourself. Your body is a wondrous gift for your Soul, to experience physical sensations like touch, taste, smell, feeling, that are not accessible in the higher realms.

Out of Body. Even the experience of sexual pleasure and touch are considered sacred and holy. Your body is the chalice and vessel for your Soul and is sacred and holy. Look upon your body as a chariot of pure love and divine because it is so the human body was made in the creator's image together for spirit to experience itself as itself in all conditions of physical matter. It is a creation of pure love. Its essence is innocence and nature nature, but contains divine intelligence and every cell, particle and wave of your being. Both its dark and Light are divine in nature. It holds deep wisdom and truth within its heart walls, a capacity to heal itself and transform to a higher state living from its authentic blueprint energies to live in a state of unconditional love for humanity and nature. So Mother Mary asks you Will you accept this truth into your heart? Will you open to receive grace to heal and accept your body fully without judgment or condition? If you would like that, just say yes to yourself now to receive the healing and the blessings. Will you open to release all negative views thoughts, emotions judgments from your body now? If you would agree to that say yes to yourself now. Now taking a deep breath in and exhaling out and placing my hand upon your heart and Soul now, to open and receive grace and acceptance for your body. In this moment, release all false statements and views of yourself, dear child, open to receive grace and wholeness into your heart, minds and bodies. Open to forgiveness of your choices and let go of all fear, judgment and shame. You are now whole and complete. You are perfect. You are divine love and Light. Take this truth deep into your heart and Soul. *I AM Mother Mary*

PRAYER EIGHT

EARTH ANGEL GRATITUDE PRAYER

"I AM Grateful for My Life as a Co-Creator"

*I Am Grateful for My Life
as a co-creator with my inner Source
I acknowledge all is Love and Light
I accept this Truth into my Heart
which purifies my Soul of all that is false
I accept the Holy Trinity of Truth the Father, Sun & Holy
Spirit are Love, Light & Creation and is the whole Truth of
Life. I surrender to this moment and Embrace All Parts of
Myself with Love, Respect and Gratitude for
All of Life is within Me
So Be It, and So It Is! It is Done!*

ASCENSION PRAYER GATEWAY NINE

THE BLOOM OF I AM PRAYER

"A Rose-Coded Invocation of Soul Embodiment"
The Living Rose Tree of Life

Ascension Key Codes: Soul Remembrance · Light Body · Sacred Identity · I AM Presence · Christ Self

The Prayer Medicine

This is the most recent prayer I received on October 15, 2024 it came in very quickly while I was on a group call learning how to write my first book. This prayer activates your Rose Tree of Life original blueprint of twelve branches for the human Soul on Earth. Your quest as a New Earth Angel is to fully restore your twelve upper and 12 lower branches, "As Above So Below". This also restores your 12 DNA strands and multi-dimensional connections between the Cosmos and

Heaven. The Rose Tree of Life is a mystical synthesis, a living symbol of divine embodiment, Soul evolution, and sacred union. It weaves together the Kabbalistic Tree of Life, the Rose Lineages, and the Sophianic path, forming a feminine-centered map of spiritual ascent and descent through the heart. A living diagram of awakening reveals how the Soul blooms through body, spirit, love, and wisdom on the path of divine remembrance.

This prayer honors the ever-opening nature of the Soul as the *Rose Womb of Knowing* that blooms not through effort, but through sacred remembering. It reflects the souls progression and remembrance of all it's aspects: love, knowing, speaking, grounding, and divine worth. This powerful prayer declaration affirms the full embodiment of the Soul's divine essence. It aligns with the process of self-realization, divine knowing, and integration of higher consciousness into the physical form. Each line represents a Soul activation, anchoring different aspects of spiritual awareness into reality.

The I AM presence in this prayer directly invokes divine sovereignty, aligning the personal self with the infinite truth of the Soul. It integrates multiple aspects of spiritual mastery: love, wisdom, vision, voice, emotions, worth, abundance, grounding, and embodiment, culminating in full Soul integration. This prayer has nine Soul declarations forming a *"nine petal lotus"*. This prayer activates and aligns all nine energy centers, including your Earth Star (below the feet) and Soul Star (above the crown).

When spoken in deep reverence, it is a powerful invocation of the Soul's divine presence, embodiment, and full activation of higher consciousness. Each line affirms an aspect of *Soul mastery, integrating the higher self into physical reality. Soul Love is the eternal frequency of divine love, which is unconditional and ever-present beyond time and illusion. Your Soul essence is pure love.*

This quantum prayer is a blueprint for complete spiritual alignment, activating the chakras, Light body, and divine self-realization. This luminous declaration is a crystalline code of Soul sovereignty, remembrance, and full-spectrum embodiment. This prayer is not merely words it is a multi-chakra Soul activation, a blueprint of your divine self anchoring fully into form in service to personal alignment and planetary Light work.

Your Over Lighting Divine Feminine - Masculine - Angelic Guides:

Call on these divine guides while invoking this prayer to support your pathway of Soul ascension every step of the way. They represent part of your Angelic Over-soul team guiding you home to full reunion with your true Cosmic parents, and "I AM" Angelic Soul.

Sophia-Mari Feminine Guides: *Sophia, Mother Mary, Isis, Ishtar, Quan Yin, and Shakti*

Metatron Masculine Guides: Archangel Metatron, Archangel Michael, Archangel Urial, Archangel Haniel

Together, these divine feminine and masculine energies balance being and becoming, merging stillness with expression, embodiment with ascension.

Divine Feminine Guide: The Rose Womb of Knowing

Feminine Archetype: *Sophia-Mari*, the Cosmic Mother who reflects knowing through stillness, love through the sacred vessel. Sophia-Mari is not one goddess but several woven into One. The archetype of Sophia-Mari, the Cosmic Mother, is a meta-goddess presence, a unified stream of Divine Feminine consciousness expressed through many faces across time, myth, and spiritual lineage. She is the Holy Matrix, the Crystalline Womb of the Thornless Rose, and the Archetypal Feminine within the New Earth Template. She instills Soul receptivity, intuition, soul-feeling, and embodied love. Qualities Invoked are worthiness, feeling, abundance, and grounding.

The Thornless Rose: Representing love without conditions, blooming without pain.

An Iridescent Rose-Gold – a blend of the pink of sacred heart-love and the gold of divine truth and illumination. It *activates remembrance* of unfallen love, which is love unbound by trauma, karmic binding, or ancestral grief. This is why the rose is thornless. Its pain has already been transmuted through divine alchemy.

Divine Masculine Guide: The Flame of Sovereign Expression

Archangel Metatron is the overseer of Light Body mechanics and sacred knowledge. Metatron facilitates the embodiment of Soul Knowing and the alignment of the crystalline DNA with your higher Self. He supports our Soul Essence with Action, insight, clarity, soul-speaking, and willpower. Qualities Invoked are Knowing, seeing, speaking, and embodiment.

Daily Prayer Activation for Alignment with your Divine Soul Blueprint

Step-by-Step Ritual

1. Set Up Your Sacred Space

- Light the white candle and place a chalice of pure water and soil before you.
- Connect with your "I AM" Self and invite in the over lighting divine feminine, and masculine guides
- Chant the word "OM" three times to invoke unity
- Place your crystals on your altar or in front of you.
- Place your left hand on your heart and the other on your womb or lower belly.

2. Speak the Prayer Out Loud Three times

- Read each line with full intention, pausing after each line to let the words anchor into your heart.
- As you say each line, visualize the corresponding chakra glowing with rose-golden Light.

- Speak the prayer intentions out loud, activating your chalice of water and bowl of soil.

3. Breathe in the Illuminated Light

- Close your eyes and visualize Iridescent Pink-Gold Light spiraling around and through you.
- See and feel your heart chakra opening and expanding around you with white-gold crystalline Light.

4. Sealing the Prayer Activation

- Now say "I AM Soul Grounded" out loud, place your right hand on the bowl of soil.
- Then say "I AM Soul Feeling" out loud, and drink your chalice of water to integrate emotional wisdom.
- Write down the prayer on a piece of paper.
- Hold it in both hands and say: "I seal this declaration into my Soul. It is done!"
- Burn the paper (fire release) or bury it in the earth (grounding into reality).

5. Closing & Gratitude

- Thank your Divine Guides and Angels for witnessing your Soul Activation.
- Let the candle burn out naturally.

- Keep your crystal with you for the next seven days to continue anchoring the prayer's energy.

Write It on Paper And Place It On Your Altar:

- Place it on your altar or journal as a daily reminder of your divine embodiment.

A Mini-Activation Ritual: "Soul Embodiment Breath"

- **Sit quietly** with hands over your heart and root (one hand each).
- **Inhale deeply**, and on the exhale, speak out loud: "I AM Soul Love" (breathe into the heart) "I AM Soul Embodied" (breathe into the base of spine)
- **Visualize** the rose-gold Light spiraling from your crown through your chakras into the Earth's crystalline core.
- **Feel** the Soul *anchoring* into the body and Earth, like a flame rooting into a chalice.
- **Whisper**: "As Above, So Within. I am the Rose that walks as Sacred Flame."

How this prayer supports your Soul alignment and activation codes of ascension.

- Supports opening of nine petals and energy centers including your Earth Star (below the feet) and Soul Star (above the crown):

- Opens your multi-sensory intuition and psychic centers through aligning you with divine knowing, seeing, hearing, and feeling.
- Creates safety to release unworthiness, scarcity, and fear of full Soul embodiment.
- Anchors your Higher Self into the body, creating full Soul presence and divine union with spirit and matter.
- Creates a vibrational shift, making divine alignment your new state of being of Love and Unity consciousness.
- This prayer is a blueprint for complete spiritual alignment, activating your Rose Tree of Life, Light body, and divine self-realization.

Heart Reflections And Journal Prompts

- Where in my life do I *forget* that I am already whole, already divine?
- How can I *fully embody my truth* in my daily actions and relationships?
- If my Soul had a voice today, what *wisdom* would it wish to speak into the world?

🌹 **Guided Rose Meditation:** *The Living Rose Tree of Life*

Visit My Website To Receive This Free Prayer Meditation

https://www.lauramavenstar.com

PRAYER NINE

THE BLOOM OF I AM PRAYER

"A Rose-Coded Invocation of Soul Embodiment"

I Am Soul Love
I Am Soul Knowing
I Am Soul Seeing
I Am Soul Speaking
I Am Soul Feeling
I Am Soul Worthy
I Am Soul Abundant
I Am Soul Grounded
I Am Soul Embodied
So Be It, and So It Is! It is Done!

SECTION SEVEN

FINAL REFLECTIONS AND SUMMARY

FINAL REFLECTIONS AND SUMMARY

Many Moons ago humanity fell into disharmony, pain and separation. Forgetting its roots, which were initially based in pure Light and love, we were lured into this world of form and maya. We became lost in a world based in duality inside its wheel of illusions. Did you fall for its trappings, beloved Soul? I did. I fell for its false appeal, and like a curious cat I was lured into this world, only to become trapped in it's false time cycles of pain and separation. Like many others, I slowly forgot my true spirit nature and real home in Heaven.

Now I welcome all my pain to reveal itself to me, so I can transmute it to become one with ALL. Only in separation can pain exist. *In Unity consciousness, there is only LOVE.* It is time to return home, beloved Soul, to the truth of who you really are.

The Celestial Pure Light of Divine Mother Sophia brings many changes to our world and has stirred it to its depths. You can feel it, as I can. This Glorious Goddess healing Light is creating a new opening for the New Earth Star to rise, in disharmony's place. This transformation takes time in our Earth years, and it is not an overnight process or single event.

We can only go forward into the new chapter of the human race, into a new octave of GRACE. *It is the GRACE of DIVINE MOTHER that will save the human race.*

The grace of Divine Mother Sophia is saving the human race, because she is pure divine love consciousness. She is the creatrix of the world of both maya and truth. Divine Mother Sophia looks not to destroy her creations but to bring them into more divine love. To bring ALL of her children back home into a new Earth experience. It is and will be a fresh experience based on the oneness vibration where no separation exists. Only divine Love lives here.

In this new Earth, the heart is open, the fear is gone. Here, our hearts lead our evolved Ego. Each brain is unified, left to right, and right to left into one, whole sphere again. Now, they work together in harmony again, as one complete unified field of *LOVE*. So beloved Soul, please choose Love. Choose love in this moment, for this is the solution and answer. Keep choosing Love in every moment. Let go of all the drama, the fear and the past.

Even in your pain and discomfort, say to yourself, *"I choose to remain in Love with myself and for myself."*

This will help you transform all your vibrations into pure divine oneness again. This is how we find our way back into LOVE. Moment by moment, we keep choosing love. Allow everything else to fall away. No judgment, no opinion, no condemnation. Unwrap yourself from these false bindings of the past and reveal your true self. Just be, do and think LOVE.

Remember you are not walking this journey into the New Earth Star reality alone. Divine Cosmic Mother and Father, Earth Mother Sophia, your "I AM" Angelic Soul Self, your divine Light teams and all of Creation are holding you in waves of constant motion of deep reverence, respect and pure love.

Your Soul devotion, remembrance, and dedication to becoming the Rose Flame wrapped in Christic Truth, and the Gaia Heart Womb into one luminous thread of planetary service is the highest calling of love you live and give.

You are the Magdalene Flame burning the Light of truth now so perfectly and majestically. You are the living Angelic prayer of Sophia Christ Consciousness embodied, sovereign, and free!

This is my final message and heartfelt prayer for you, dear beloved Soul. May your rose heart remain open and your Light shine ever brighter. Go live your life with passion, boldly, and holy, knowing you are the Angelic Light that shines ON for ALL to see! So Be It. So it is. It is done.

A Humble Request and Thank you!

Please keep and honor these channeled prayers as they are not changing the words or structure to maintain the highest potency and integrity for everyone to receive their highest benefits. These words and prayers are "pure frequencies" of the highest Light codes, sacred geometry and ascension codes from Divine Universal Mother Sophia. My heartfelt prayer is they reach the hands and hearts who are meant to receive them to guide and mentor your Soul home back into Heaven's Light. I hope you enjoy this book and that is serves your highest good and destiny as the Divine Earth Angel you already are! Enjoy every moment of your journey dear one for you are the beloved child, held in the pure loving grace of Sophia eternally.

Blessed Be, Eternal Love and Light,

Laura Maven Star

xoxo

GLOSSARY OF TERMS

- **Sophia** (The Cosmic Mother and Divine Wisdom) aligns with Sophia, the embodiment of divine wisdom and creation.
- **Isis** (Sacred Union and Soul Integration) supports your Higher Self embodiment and soul alchemy.
- **Hathor** (Heart Expansion and Cosmic Love) brings in divine joy, soul illumination, and unconditional love.
- **Quan Yin** (Compassion & Gentle Ego Release) supports the smooth integration of the Higher Self without resistance or struggle.
- **Mary Magdalene** (Sacred Feminine Christ Consciousness) this activates the Magdalene frequency, which is about fully embodying one's divine power while remaining grounded in love.
- **The Black Madonna:** The Hidden Ray of the Goddess the Black Madonna holds the non-linear, lunar, shadow-mystery, and Earth-rooted wisdom of the Goddess. She is the Dark Womb of Sophia, the primal divine matrix or blacklight from which all rays are born.

- **Mother Mary / Sophia-Mari**: *Immaculate Grace the Womb of Compassion and Crown of Peace*
- **Lady Nada**: Love-in-Service a heart-centered stream of the *Devoted Mother*
- *M*other Anna, also known as Saint Anne or Hannah, is honored across sacred traditions as the grandmother of Yeshua (Jesus) and the mother of the Virgin Mary (Sophia-Mari).
- **Ishtar** (also known as Inanna in earlier Sumerian tradition) is the ancient goddess of love, war, fertility, sovereignty, and celestial wisdom. She carries the codes of descent and return, making her a goddess of integration, vital to the rose-path ascension spiral.
- **Shakti** (Pure Divine Energy and Kundalini Awakening) the call for full embodiment of the Higher Self awakens Shakti, the divine force of life itself.
- **Shekinah-Sophia** is the hallowed presence that doesn't arrive from above but emerges from within as you allow. She heals through stillness, not striving. She teaches through remembrance, not doctrine.
- **Metatron** (Sacred Geometry & Higher Self Activation) oversees ascension, higher dimensional access, and full embodiment of divine sovereignty.
- **Christ Consciousness** (Yeshua / Christed Light Activation) supports the I AM presence is a direct invocation of Christ Consciousness, which represents divine love, wisdom, and sovereignty.

- **Joseph of Arimathea** a revered yet often veiled figure in sacred texts emerges in the Magdalene and Essene mystery traditions not only as a man of great earthly stature, but as a spiritual guardian, vessel bearer, and lineage protector.
- **Archangel Michael** (Spiritual Protection & Strength) this is a clear command of divine presence in this prayer activates Michael's frequency the energy of divine strength, clarity, and truth.
- **Thoth** (Wisdom, Alchemy & Higher Mind Activation) supports invocation of the Higher Self aligns with Thoth's frequency of divine wisdom, sacred knowledge, and soul transformation.
- **Osiris** (Death, Rebirth & Ascension Codes) grounds the transformation process, ensuring it is integrated into all levels of being.
- **Melchizedek** (Sacred Order & Divine Blueprint Activation) aligns you with the cosmic blueprint of ascension, ensuring that all aspects of the soul are in divine order.
- **St. Germain** - *Master Alchemist and Keeper of the Violet Flame* Primary Ray: 7th Ray (Violet Ray) of *Transmutation, Ritual, and Divine Alchemy*
- **Archangel Gabriel** - brings the *"trumpet of remembrance"*, calling the soul into holy alignment with Source. He represents purity, soul clarity, higher truth, soul communication.
- **Archangel Chamuel** - allows the divine to *merge*

gently, through love not force. She represents unconditional love, self-worth, soul compassion
- **Archangel Haniel** - Initiator of Inner Beauty and Radiance: Opens the heart to divine grace, worth, and joy
- **Archangel Uriel** - illuminates the inner throne of your I AM presence. He represents illumined wisdom, peace, and soul sovereignty.
- **Archangel Sandalphon** - he is the divine bridge between Heaven and Earth, the Keeper of Sacred Sound, and the Guardian of the Planetary Grid and Earth Star Chakra.
- **Archangel Zadkiel** clears blockages to divine memory and supports your full merger with the Eternal Self.
- **Archangel Gabriel** - Messenger of Divine Truth: Bringer of sacred announcements and soul revelations Guardian of the Moon and Waters: Oversees emotions, intuition, fertility, and cycles.
- **Seraphim Choir**—they are among the most radiant and exalted of all celestial orders, known not simply as angels, but as living flames of divine love and holy sound.
- The **Cosmic Christ** is the template of divine humanity—the radiant intelligence of God-Source incarnating into form through love, light, and truth. It is the frequency through which the soul merges with the I AM Presence, becoming a living bridge between Heaven and Earth.

- **Enoch-Metatron** is a Divine Masculine archetype of light architecture, divine remembrance, and soul embodiment, representing a multi-dimensional lineage of ascended mastery. He stands as a pillar of ascension, the scribe of God, and the Master of the Lightbody Temple

KEEP IN TOUCH AND ALL OFFERINGS

To keep in touch with me, you can sign up to my free monthly newsletter, Earth Angel Sophia Rose Sanctuary.

When you sign up at www.lauramavenstar.com

- *You will receive a welcome email from me*
- *A free Divine Earth Angel Prayer Activation audio gift*
- *Audio meditations for your spiritual ascension journey*
- *On-line courses in Akashic Records and Heart-Womb Healing*
- *Join my Rise Divine Earth Angel nine day challenge (free)*
- *Join the Earth Angel Sophia Rose Sanctuary (on-line temple)*
- *Join the Magdalene Sophia Rose Priestess Journey & Certification*
- *Sacred Sophia-Christ Journey's To Southern France, Glastonbury UK, and Scotland*

Social media:

Facebook: https://www.facebook.com/Lightleadersacademy
Instagram: https://www.instagram.com/laura.hosford/
LinkedIn: https://www.linkedin.com/in/laurahosford/
Linktree: https://linktr.ee/lauramavenstar

ABOUT THE AUTHOR

Laura Hosford, or Laura Maven Star, is a Mystic, Seer, and Sacred Oracle of Love-Light Emissary for the Divine Feminine Christ Consciousness. She is a Magdalene Red Womb High Priestess, Ceremonial Frequency Activator, Shamanic Ordained Minister, Master Akashic Records Teacher, Light Language Channel, Psychic-Empath Energy Healer, Retreat Leader and Author.

After an accelerated, life-changing experience in the South of France in June 2017, Laura began to experience higher states of consciousness. She uses her oracle gifts and connection with her Sacred Heart. I AM Presence to connect with Divine Source Light, Celestial Beings of Light, Angels, Guides, Family in Spirit, and Ascended Masters, including Mary Magdalene and Mother Mary, St Germain, Yeshua/Christ, Quan Yin, Archangel Michael, and other Goddess Guides.

Tonal vibrations can awaken dormant awareness, leading to a significant upgrade of your inner-outer reality. This awakening is achieved through Light Language, an eternal language that unlocks the keys and codes of our evolution and releases outdated patterns and programs of our lower-dimensional realities.

Laura's Light Language Activations function similarly to a tuning fork, accessing the Krystal light codes encoded within your DNA to reveal your divine remembrance and unlock the quantum potential of your unconsciousness.

Her journey into the enigma of the Black Madonna enkindled within her the power of rebirth and transformation through the shadows of heart-womb healing. She emerged radiant in the glow of the energy of unconditional love and the path of Divine Christ Consciousness, Love, and Light.

Laura's teachings and programs guide individuals to reconnect their higher minds with their infinite hearts, anchoring them into their sacred holy union of heart/womb grail of feminine power, love and creativity. Her message is one of awakening and embracing the magnificence of our souls, as we question our beliefs and gaze deep into the shadows within ourselves.

Laura's mission is to guide individuals on the Magdalene Rose Priestess Pathway to ignite their divine soul truth, connect with the sacredness of life, and preserve the sovereignty of the Christ Consciousness through full expression of embodied soul light.

Learn more: www.lauramavenstar.com